Ethical Practice in Child and Adolescent Analysis and Psychotherapy

Ethical Practice in Child and Adolescent Analysis and Psychotherapy

Protecting Safety in a Therapeutic Environment

Anita G. Schmukler, Paula G. Atkeson, Helene Keable, and E. Kirsten Dahl

JASON ARONSON
Lanham • Boulder • New York • Toronto • Plymouth, UK

Published by Jason Aronson
A wholly owned subsidiary of The Rowman & Littlefield Publishing Group, Inc.
4501 Forbes Boulevard, Suite 200, Lanham, Maryland 20706
www.rowmanlittlefield.com

Estover Road, Plymouth PL6 7PY, United Kingdom

British Library Cataloguing in Publication Information Available

Library of Congress Cataloging-in-Publication Data

Library of Congress Cataloging-in-Publication Data Available
ISBN 978-0-7657-0818-2 (cloth : alk. paper) -- ISBN 978-0-7657-0820-5 (electronic)

™ The paper used in this publication meets the minimum requirements of American National Standard for Information Sciences Permanence of Paper for Printed Library Materials, ANSI/NISO Z39.48-1992.

Printed in the United States of America

The rich and insightful clinical discussions held in our committee on psychoanalytic education study group on supervision in child and adolescent analysis, over the years, prompted us to write this volume. The study group members contributed their clinical wisdom and penetrating questions to our exploration of ethical practice in clinical work. The authors thank the study group members for their immeasurable contributions to this volume. The authors are solely responsible for the material and opinions which appear in this volume.

Contents

Preface

Historical Perspective: Ethical Issues in Psychoanalytic and Psychodynamic Therapies of Children and Adolescents—A Selective Literature Review

The current renewed interest in ethical issues in the clinical practice of psychotherapy and psychoanalysis has its foundations in a long tradition. The Hippocratic Oath, from its original version to later adaptations to changing values, addresses two fundamental ethical staples: practicing within the limits of one's competencies and never doing harm. It states, "I will prescribe regimens for the good of my patients according to my ability and judgment and never do harm to anyone" (North, 2009). The asymmetry of the clinical encounter is defined by the understanding that the clinician brings to it a set of specific competencies; the importance of the clinical outcome is emphasized by the aspiration of doing no harm. Aristotle, in his *Nicomachean Ethics*, described the unique, trusting quality of the clinical relationship, which in current usage we describe as "fiduciary." For Aristotle (Aristotle, 2009), a doctor "seems not even to study health in this way [the idea of health itself], but [to study] the health of a man, or perhaps rather the health of a particular man; it is individuals that he is healing." Sigmund Freud, in his *XXVII Introductory Lecture on Psychoanalysis*, "Transference," revisits the concept of the "moral man" and contrasts the scope of the analyst's work with the tasks of the physician or the educator. As per Stratchey (1963), Freud writes,

> I can assure you that you are misinformed if you suppose that advice and guidance in the affairs of life play an integral part in analytic influence. On the contrary, so far as possible we avoid the role of a mentor such as this, and there is nothing we would rather bring about than that the patient should make his decisions for himself. Only in the case of some very youthful or quite helpless or unstable individuals are we unable to put the limitation of our role into effect.

TOWARD THE MAINTENANCE OF ETHICAL COMPETENCIES

An ethical competence implies a combination of knowledge and actions that are integrated, coordinated, and applied in specific and often unique clinical contexts. Those clinical contexts may be suffused with distinctive, unanticipated, and often conflictual situations. Ethical competencies in psychotherapy and psychoanalysis are rooted in codes of standards and ethics developed by most professional organizations. Ethical competencies have emerged and continue to dynamically evolve. In this context, the limitations of the codes of standards and ethics cannot be translated linearly into applicable and flexible permutations, which are required in the course of the complexities encountered in clinical work.

Major professional organizations (medicine, psychiatry, psychology, social work, and other mental health disciplines) have created and revised their respective codes of ethics. For example, the American Medical Association established a code of ethics and delineated the minimum requirements for medical education in 1847 at its first official meeting and, since 1980, has adopted revised principles of medical ethics to reflect professional and legal standards in a changing society (American Medical Association, 1997). Over the past two decades, the American Board of Medical Specialties and the Royal College of Physicians and Surgeons (Canada) have introduced, for all specialties, programs of maintenance of certification that describe core competencies deemed mandatory for all practitioners and researchers in medicine. For purposes of illustration the programs of maintenance of certification in adult psychiatry and child and adolescent psychiatry can be accessed at www.abpn.com. Faulkner (Faulker, 2011) and Roberts (Roberts, 2011) posit that the foundations of ethical practice constitute one, if not the major one, of the core competencies. The American Psychoanalytic Association (APsaA) has developed its own principles and standards of ethics (1975, 1983, and 1987) and its most recent version is accessible online at www.apsa.org (American Psychoanalytic Association, 2010). In addition, the American Psychoanalytic Association (American Psychoanalytic Association, 2008) has published a second edition of its *Ethics Case Book*, a recognition that competent clinical psychoanalytic practice, akin to other types of mental health practice, demands that the clinician solves in the field numerous permutations of ethical conflicts. All major principles and standards of ethics recognize that ethical problems cannot be readily codified, as they share boundaries with the development of morality, changing societal mores, and legal jurisprudence. These complexities are magnified when clinicians treat children and adolescents, as the demands of clinical work include the refined and multifaceted skills of working with families, legal guardians, other caretakers, other professionals, and third parties. Other considerations with respect to minors, such as immaturity of development, information of exchanges, working with parents, advocacy, multiple transferences, and countertransferences of child therapists, further amplify the difficulties of subtle resolution of ethical conflicts. Finally, cultural differences, conflicting theoretical stances of healers, a multitude of treatment options, and the differences in healers trained in multiple disciplines can strain the expertise of even the most able practitioners. Although the most recent edition of the APsaA *Ethics Case Book* (American Psychoanalytic Association, 2008) frequently refers to the needs of minors, there is a conspicuous lack of clinical illustrations involving children. The American Academy of Child and Adolescent Psychiatry (AACAP) developed its code of ethics in 1980 (American Academy of Child and Adolescent Psychiatry, 1980) and adopted a revision at the January 2009 Council meeting which is accessible online at www.aacap.org. Like other professional organizations, the ethics committee of the American Academy of Child and Adolescent Psychiatry has started to complement its codes of ethics by studying clinical vignettes that illustrate the multiple facets of ethical dilemmas emerging from most treatments with children and adolescents.

Teaching ethics and its application by clinical illustrations is emerging as a promising venue (Horsley, O'Neill, McGowan, Perrier, & Kane, 2011). Possibly in that spirit, the committee charged to revise the American Psychoanalytic Association 2007 *Ethics Case Book* aimed to expand awareness of these issues through stimulating formal educational offerings in psychoanalytic and psychodynamic psychotherapy curricula and by promoting the development of discussion groups at local and national meetings. The experience gathered during these various educational programs has been that specific illustrations of the general principles seem to be the most effective tool for raising awareness of the nuances of several clinical issues, and that clinical vignettes are apt to stimulate productive discussions (personal communications) (Brunkow, 2010) (Asherman & Rubin, 2010).

SEARCH METHODOLOGY

Aware of the paucity of available evidence that explores the theoretical and clinical issues of ethical practices in the praxis of psychoanalytic and psychodynamic treatments of children and adolescents, we opted for a two-step process. The first step elicits the theoretical and clinical issues surrounding current ethical work with children and adolescents; the second step sets forth specific questions illustrated in different clinical vignettes. The primary intent of the first step is the exploration of a focused search of the literature on the ethical issues pertaining to clinical practice with children and adolescents. The importance of this topic is clear for the practitioners of psychoanalysis, psychoanalytic therapies, and psychodynamic therapies.

In preparing material for this chapter, the author searched several electronic databases: Psychoanalytic Electronic Publishing (PEP-WEB), Cochrane Database of Systematic Reviews, OVID Medline, and psychINFO. These databases were searched for the following terms: psychoanalysis or psychoanalytic therapy or psychodynamic therapy, and ethics or codes of ethics, while limiting the search terms to children or adolescents. The result was a marked paucity of entries.

The idea of autonomy is at the base of all principles of ethical behavior for clinical practice (Capell, 1967) (Shor, 1961). This indicates the role of the patient's independence and self-reliance has, historically, been considered crucial in formulating ethical principles. From this perspective, psychoanalysis is anchored in the patient's achieving autonomy, which is a core ethical value. The crucial question for our purposes: to what degree do we value autonomy in child and adolescent patients? What is the link between developmental progression along lines of autonomy and development of a sense of ethics? What is the conflict between the child's developing autonomy and questions of privacy and confidentiality?

Furlong (Furlong, 2005) argues that ethical principles live in a contextual matrix that must be critically evaluated. He addresses this question by studying confidentiality with respect to third parties. These issues are addressed in detail in this text.

In addition to our examination of electronic databases, the work of a sample of analysts who have addressed, at least implicitly, principles of ethics, was reviewed: J. Chused, J. Kantrowitz, R. Karush, H. Keable, J. and K. Novick, J. Yanof, and A. Schmukler. Collectively, their work addressed various areas of competence that relate to ethical practice. These areas include: setting the analytic frame according to the stage of development (Karush, 1993) (K. Novick & Novick, 2002) (J. Novick & Novick, 2008) (Schmukler, 2006); assessing indications for starting (Schmukler, 2011) (Keable, 2002) and terminating analytic treatments (J. Novick, 1990); working within the transference or countertransference (Chused, 1988) (Olesker, 2006) (Yanof, 1996); understanding developmental needs; evaluating aspects of the analytic process and outcome (Keable, 2008), and in reflecting on ethical ways to transmit analytic material (Kantrowitz, 2004) (Kantrowitz, 2008). In spite of the implicit reference to issues of ethics, none of these authors, with the exception of Kantrowitz who works with adults, has examined, directly and explicitly, the ethical issues underpinning analytic practice.

SUMMARY OF METHODOLOGY SEARCHES AND FUTURE DIRECTIONS

This literature review reveals a serious dearth of current data and resources that could facilitate the awareness of ethical issues, specifically in the pediatric age, where contextual life issues, psychological maturation, and dependence on caretakers and institutions might highlight such issues. At a historical juncture where most institutions have developed their codes of ethics and standards, we observe a lack of translation of this written literature into the clinical work of how a clinician will recognize, in often intricate clinical scenarios, what ethical principles are present, in synergy or discordance, and how to assess systematically and critically, the resolution of such conflicts.

The paucity of data certainly does not imply that ethical issues are not addressed in psychoanalytic and psychodynamic treatment, but it certainly suggests that the time is ripe to address the issues in question more explicitly in the literature, and in other venues (as seen in the attempts offered in this book) as well as in supervisory settings and pertinent seminars. The reviewed literature offers several themes for urgent and future consideration. There is, among these, an ongoing tension in the understanding of the domain of ethics in psychoanalysis. Some consider the ethics of psychoanalysis as positing a quest for the truth at the individual level, always private and never public (Allphin, 2005). Others view psychoanalysis and psychodynamic therapies as therapeutic modalities, practiced by an array of professionals, who have to be accountable to the demands of their respective combined fields of practice (Blass, 2001). Leary (2007) underscored the necessity to build expertise and capacity for innovative thinking and the aptness of the case study to do so. This dearth of knowledge and expertise is further echoed in Merlino's (2006) opinion that ethics permeates our field today and how a revised and expanded professional ethics is critical to our future. Emerging themes of study include: the importance of ethical attitudes in the analytic relationship; the ethical and evaluative nature of developmental models in psychoanalysis; the relevance of the domain of ethics in modern practices; possible contributions of psychoanalysis to the spheres of national health care and social justice (Margolis, 2001); the need for conceptual research (Leuzinger-Bohleber & Discman, 2006); as well as process and outcome studies.

Future directions could be summarized in terms of a select few principles of practice to be considered by psychoanalysts and psychodynamic clinicians—that is, the recognition of the role of ethics in psychoanalytic education and the critical will needed to recognize, refine, and expand our understanding of professional ethics. These objectives will hopefully continue to be rooted in our long psychoanalytic tradition, yet be adapted to the demands of modern and often eclectic practices, in keeping with the values of the analytic tradition. Such directions and objectives point to the void that this case book will attempt to fill by studying the lively engagement of ethics with the clinical task.

REFERENCES

Allphin, C. (2005). An ethical attitude in the analytic relationship. *Journal of Analytic Psychology, 50*, 451–468.

American Academy of Child and Adolescent Psychiatry. (1980). *Code of Ethics*. Washington, D.C.s: The American Academy of Child and Adolescent Psychiatry.

American Medical Association. (1997). *Code of Medical Ethics Current Opinions with Annotations (150th Anniversary ed.)*. Chicago: American Medical Association.

American Psychoanalytic Association. (2008). *Ethics Case Book* (2nd ed.). New York: American Psychoanalytic Association.

American Psychoanalytic Association. (2010). *Principles and Standards of Ethics for Psychoanalysts*. www.apsa.org. Retrieved August 1, 2010.

Aristotle. (2009). *Nicomachean ethics*. New York: Oxford University Press.

Ascherman, L., & Rubin, S. (2010). Value of clinical vignettes in the work with parents. Unpublished manuscript.

Blass, R. (2001). On the ethical and evaluative nature of developmental models in psychoanalysis. *Psychoanalytic Study of the Child, 56*, 193–218.

Brunkow, C. (2010). Value of clinical vignettes. Unpublished manuscript.

Capell, M. (1967). The ethical basis for psychoanalysis. *Psychoanalytic Review, 54D*, 132–140.

Chused, J. (1988). The transference neurosis in child psychoanalysis. *Psychoanalytic Study of the Child*, 43, 51–81.

Dewald, P., & Clark, R. (Eds.). (2008). *Ethics case book of the American Psychoanalytic Association*. New York: Author.

Faulker, L. (2011). Promoting quality patient care through physician competence: applying deliberate practice to lifelong learning. *Focus, 9* (2), 165–170.

Furlong, A. (2005). Confidentiality with respect to third parties. A psychoanalytic view. *International Journal of Pyschoanalysis, 86*, 375–394.

Horsley, T., O'Neill, J., McGowan, G., Perrier, L., Kane, G., & Campbell, C. (2010). Interventions to improve question formulation in professional practice and self-directed learning. *Cochrane Effective Practice and Organization of Care Group Cochrane Database of Systematic Reviews*. 12 (5), CD007335.

Kantrowitz, J. (2004). Writing about patients: I. Ways of protecting confidentiality and analysts' conflicts over choice of method. *Journal of the American Psychoanalytic Association, 52*, 69–99.

Kantrowitz, J. (2008). Writing about patients III: 1. Comparisons of attitudes and practices of analysts residing outside and within the USA. *International Journal of Psychoanalysis, 85*, 691–712.

Karush, R. (1993). Sam: A child analysis. *Journal of Clinical Psychoanalysis, 2*, 43–61.

Keable, H. (2002). Child case presentation. *Journal of Clinical Psychoanalysis*, 11, 510–523.

Keable, H. (2008). *Defenses: a therapeutic tool and outcome measures*. Paper presented at the American Academy of Child and Adolescent Psychiatry, Norbert and Charlotte Rieger Psychodynamic Psychotherapy Award presentation.

Leary, K. (2007). "Making the case" for practical psychoanalysis. *Psychoanalytic psychology, 34*, 701–708.

Leuzinger-Bohleber, M., & Fischmann, T. (2006). What is conceptual research in psychoanalysis? *International Journal of Psychoanalysis, 87*, 1355–1386.

Margolis, M. (2001). The American Psychoanalytic Association: A decade of change. *Journal of the American Psychoanalytic Association, 49*, 11–25.
Merlino, J. (2006). Psychoanalysis and ethics—relevant then, essential now. *Journal of the American Academy of Psychoanalysis, 34*, 231–247.
North, M. (2009). The Hippocratic Oath. www.nlm.nih.gov/hmd/greek/greek_oath.html (Retrieved August 1,2011).
Novick, J. (1990). Comments on termination in child, adolescent and adult analysis. *Psychoanalytic Study of the Child, 45*, 419–436.
Novick, J., & Novick, K. (2008). Expanding the domain privacy, secrecy and confidentiality. *Annals of Psychoanalysis, 36*, 146–160.
Novick, K., & Novick, J. (2002). Reclaiming the land. *Psychoanalytic Psychology, 19*, 348–377.
Olesker, W. (2006). Thoughts on medications and psychoanalysis: A lay analyst's view. *Journal of the American Psychoanalytic Association, 54*, 763–779.
Roberts, L. (2011). Case studies in ethics. *Focus, 9* (2), 197.
Schmukler, A. (2006). How analysts think, and why they think the way they do; reflections on three analytic hours. Book review. *Journal of the American Psychoanalytic Association, 54*, 343–346.
Schmukler, A. (2011). *When analysis is indispensable.* Paper presented at the Annual Meeting of the American Psychoanalytic Association.
Shor, J. (1961). The ethic of Freud's psychoanalysis—reflections on Freud. The mind of the moralist by Philip Rieff. *International Journal of Psychoanalysis, 42*, 116–122.
Strachey, J. (1963). *The standard edition of the complete psychological works of Sigmund Freud* (Vol. 16). London: Hogarth Press.
Yanof, J. (1996a). Language, communication and transference in child analysis. I. Selective mutism: The medium is the message. *Journal of the American Psychoanalytic Association, 44*, 79–100.
Yanof, J. (1996b). Language, communication and transference in child analysis. II. Is child analysis really child analysis? *Journal of the American Psychoanalytic Association, 44*, 79–116.

Introduction

This volume addresses crucial and perplexing questions of ethical practice which arise in our psychotherapeutic work with children, adolescents, and their parents. Ethical practice describes the desired behavior of the analyst or therapist with the child patient, parents, and all others with whom the therapist might come into contact. It involves relationship and it presupposes behavior that is conducted with honesty, integrity, reliability, maintenance of a stable structure for the treatment, and a clear view of avoiding potential for harm.

Why is the matter of ethical practice relevant in the treatment of children? For one thing, since a child is considered a "minor," her/his best interests are frequently overlooked in therapeutic settings, since initial dialogue typically takes place between parent or guardian and therapist. The position of "minor" also finds expression in psychological thinking. Parents want to find relief for their child (who may be suffering), themselves, and the other children in the family. In some instances, the "voice" of the child in question is lost, especially in terms of considering approaches to treatment.

Curiously, when therapeutic ethical codes are presented and discussed with respect to "patients," scant attention is given to work with children and adolescents. Hence, the need for this volume. The topics addressed here were stimulated by a series of highly productive discussions of the Study Group on Supervision in Child Analysis, which was sponsored by the Committee on Psychoanalytic Education of the American Psychoanalytic Association. The participants, all supervisors of child analysis, met semi-annually for several years and each presented to the group some of the dilemmas they encountered in their supervision of psychoanalytic candidates. During the course of our work, it became evident that many of the clinical issues that we discussed had components that involved setting boundaries, and some of these dilemmas included matters of ethical practices. It also became abundantly clear that the written presentation of our work would be helpful not only to child analysts, but to all clinicians and students who treat children and their parents and are eager for illumination of these perplexing problems.

As we began to examine the psychoanalytic literature, we were all struck by the relative paucity of material that set forth and examined ethical principles in treating children and working with their parents. *Case Book on Ethics*, published by the American Psychoanalytic Association, contains detailed material about ethical practice in working with adults, but addresses very little with respect to ethical dilemmas that arise in working with children and their parents. Rubin and Ascherman have written a paper, unpublished, that addresses some aspects of ethical practice in working with children and their parents.

The American Psychological Association, the American Academy of Child and Adolescent Psychiatry, and the National Association of Social Workers has each codified standards for their respective disciplines. Each has set forth, to some degree, specific issues of ethical dilemmas in working with children.

In various chapters in this volume, we examine the reasons (conscious and unconscious) for the development of the guidelines, or "rules." Understanding that which leads to formulation of rules is helpful in our efforts to work with clinical material.

The preface in this volume provides a literature review. With respect to ethical standards set forth by various psychological organizations, we encourage the interested reader to consider the motives for such ethical codes. While behavioral suggestions are useful, they are most likely to be carried out if there is an understanding of the motives for ethical breaches and the reasons for establishing "rules."

Following the review of literature, the first chapter addresses various clinical models, and includes a variety of ways of understanding that take place in a therapy session. For example, we found that while one therapist might consider that attending a child's birthday party might simply be "natural," another might consider attending the party as a "corrective emotional experience." And yet another therapist might view this as a boundary crossing. There is a wide variety of clinical material that can be viewed from multiple perspectives, and this subject will be examined in depth in the chapter.

Despite these differences, the similarities in thinking about ethical practice in working with children were sufficiently substantive that we felt the topic worthy of a monograph that would be useful to therapists who work from a wide variety of perspectives.

Our chapter on transference and countertransference addresses the unconscious forces that shape the relationships of therapist and child and therapist and parents. In this context, unique ethical issues arise. The child therapist and analyst speaks not simply with her/his patient (as does the therapist of adults) but may also communicate with parents, at times, with teachers, clergy, divorce attorneys, and an array of others. This adds a particular burden to the work of the child therapist, since the impact of communication with others who are participants in the child's life is frequently not examined and not well understood. Our knowledge of the child's ways of reacting to her/his therapist's contact with outsiders is enriched when our understanding includes not simply observing the child's responses but our awareness that the child's unconscious reactions may simultaneously contribute to the ways in which he/she responds. Our capacity to understand and work with the child's feelings, in this context, may profoundly affect the child's trust in her/his therapist.

In this context, the therapist, too, has unconscious responses (transferences and counter transferences) to those with whom she/he communicates during the course of treatment, such as unexplained anger with the parents, competition with the child (or the parent), or unexplained libidinal responses. The awareness of the presence of unconscious forces can help the child therapist to seek counsel in advance of confronting a challenging issue.

The therapist of children deals with multiple transferences and frequently is unaware of the nature of the difficulties. Symptoms appear in sleepiness during sessions with children (see chapter on transferences for discussion of this), anger with parents, unconscious identification with the child or with parent, punitive feelings toward the child, competitive behavior with either the child or parents, and intense emotional involvement that seems, at the time, incomprehensible.

Since work with a child of a particular age may stir conflicts in the therapist related to his/her own development at that age, both an awareness of this fact and careful examination of the therapist's responses to the child's behavior and feelings may help to deal with obstacles and challenges in the treatment.

Failure to engage in this form of self-reflection in repsonse to apparent provocations may interfere with empathy and deeper understanding and may leave the therapist more vulnerable to his unconcious conflicts. This example is one demonstration that clinical skill and ethical practice are inextricably interwoven. Given multiple such examples, the authors of this volume decided it might be useful for students, teachers, and supervisors to have the opportunity to use a workbook to generate useful discussion that would advance our work with children.

In this text, we are offering a kind of preventive work in our suggestion that unconscious factors be acknowledged and addressed. What of the child who expresses that he/she has "no interest" in what transpires during our meeting with parents? We must attend to these matters continually and, if they fail to arise directly, look for them in derivative form in the play. For example, a young child shows no interest in our having met with parents earlier today, yet play involves a stuffed bear who has a "big mouth" and lacks discretion. Often the derivative material is not so blatant and clinical skill is required to detect references that might easily go unnoticed, thus compromising a potentially trusting relationship.

In our chapter on working with parents, we address particular challenges of working with parents of children whom we treat. It includes issues of privacy, secrecy, and working with the parents' transferences to the therapist and with the therapist's transferences and countertransferences to the parents. We help parents to understand what their child is confronting, without disclosing direct material from the treatment. We also help them to understand their envy of the child (when it is present), and their narcissistic injury over having to ask for treatment for a young child. "Where did we go wrong?" they might lament. And we help them to work with feelings that their child, temporarily, is speaking of private matters to a relative stranger, while the child may not be sharing that material with their parents. Parents must understand that the situation is a temporary one and, in respecting their child's privacy, they are helping development to move forward.

When the parents provide historical material to the therapist or analyst, he or she may have various notions of the degree to which they wish to be included in the child's treatment. Does the parent imagine that he/she should be included in every session? Does she/he wish to hear about every word that the child, with feelings of trust, conveyed to the therapist? How does the therapist learn to negotiate with parents who want their child treated but have difficulty in recognizing that the child's sharing in privacy with a trusted therapist must be respected? Is the parent having difficulty relinquishing perceived control over his/her child? Is the wish to "control" the therapy part of the effort to maintain an infantile tie with the child in treatment? We address these, and many other, issues in the chapter on working with parents.

Chapter 4, on supervision of therapy with children and their parents, examines ways to work with both the novice and the experienced therapist who consult with us to examine blind spots and improve the quality of the therapy they offer to children and parents. In our study of working with students of child psychotherapy and psychoanalysis, we found that the greatest risks for ethical problems took place when the student or therapist seeking consultation was unaware of his/her motives, feelings, goals, responses, and defenses. When the therapist seeking consultation becomes aware of her/his impulses, wishes, hopes, and fears, his/her work becomes more effective and the tendencies to engage in acting-out behavior become diminished markedly.

An additional locus of our study has been the role of the supervisor in child and adolescent therapy and the transferences and countertransferences that takes place during the supervisory experience. Failure to attend to unconscious elements in the supervisor-supervisee relationship may interfere both with the candidate's learning and with her/his ability to function as an effective clinician. The patient suffers.

The supervisory experience requires continual examination, on the part of both participants. Unexamined problematic issues may lead to unconscious acting out, with both child-patient and parent. When this takes place, and narcissistic issues prevail, there may be a tendency to overlook ethical principles. At this juncture, we underscore the fact that many of these categories overlap, and the chapter on supervision will also include material related to transferences and countertransferences.

In chapter 5, on forensics, we examine the effect on a child's treatment when the therapist is asked to submit records to divorce attorneys for settlement of legal manners. Should the therapist be involved in disclosing privileged material? What is the effect of this upon an ongoing treatment of a child or adolescent? If boundaries are interrupted, damaged or severed because of legal issues, might that child be unable to engage not simply with the current therapist but with all future therapists?

In chapter 6, on writing about clinical material, we address the ways in which the analyst or therapist thinks about publication of clinical material that involves analysis or therapy. What's the value of our community to read this material and what is the potential impact on the child patient of asking permission for publication? What is the impact upon a child or adolescent who discovers his published case history on the internet, when his parents, years earlier, gave permission for this to take place? At what point should the child's perspective be considered? Does this relate purely to age or to stage of development? From an ethical perspective, how does the supervisor help the child's therapist to think about including the child in these decisions?

Chapter 7 is pivotal, as it examines and delineates, in a substantive way, the vulnerability of the therapist of children and parents to ethical dilemmas. This is particularly true when the therapist's awareness of the impact of unconscious material on her/his interactions with child patients and parents is given insufficient attention.

The final chapter is a summary of essential clinical and theoretical material that we hope to convey. This includes work in our practice as well as what we attempt to convey in teaching and supervision.

Our appendix includes suggested outlines for a course in ethical practice in working with children and their parents. This outline might serve for courses, seminars, discussion groups, and even work in supervision.

While training programs for adult analysts and therapists include courses on ethics, this has not been true for training in work with children. The need for such discussion, from early in training, appears to be crucial.

We hope this text serves as a form of workbook and raises many questions for discussion. We shall not attempt to answer every individual issue raised, although many are examined, from differing vantage points, in more than one chapter. Our hope is to generate questions for discussion in classrooms, workshops, seminars, supervisory hours, and clinical conferences. We suggest that the interested reader keep a notebook in which he/she lists and examines both ethical dilemmas that have been previously unrecognized, potential ethical problems, and ways these problematic issues might be approached. Peer supervision, consultation, and personal therapy can help the interested therapist to examine difficulties and make changes that benefit child and adolescent patients, their parents, and their therapists.

Ethical practice dictates that we respect our relationships with our child and adolescent patients and their parents. The significance of this must not be overestimated, and it determines the freedom that our child patients experience in sharing their struggles with their therapist or analyst. A prerequisite for an effective treatment is that our patients, however young, experience full freedom of communicating with a trusted therapist. In all medical offices today, patients are asked to sign a document that indicates that they understand "privacy laws." However, full comprehension of this, as it relates to psychotherapeutic work with children and adolescents, is often not present. At times, therapists who have little awareness of the impact of unconscious pressures upon their work, may, in their efforts to please parents, have difficulty in grasping the crucial impact upon a treatment of protecting privacy of children while simultaneously respecting the perceived needs of parents.

The common assumption that ethical practice is limited to boundary issues is limited in scope. From a more comprehensive perspective, we must include decisions about treatment modalities, including psychopharmacology and diagnosis as well.

How does the therapist address the ethical issues in working with parents who request a particular diagnosis (albeit not the correct one) because they believe that presenting this diagnosis to a school may be the only way that their child might receive much needed services in an educational context? What of the parent who insists upon medication for the child when, in the therapist's clinical judgment, effective psychotherapy could resolve the problem, although it might take a bit longer? To what degree do therapists "compromise," by offering medication to a child to pacify the parent, teacher, or insurance company, although this is not indicated clinically? What are the ethical principles that guide us in thinking about such dilemmas? What is the effect upon our child patient when a treatment modality is instituted that is largely for the purpose of pacifying parents? What is the effect upon the therapist who abandons her/his principles of treatment in order to satisfy demands of persons other than the patient? For example, if an insurance company has a single criterion, symptom disappearance, and this can be accomplished, at least temporarily, by medication, what demands does this place on the therapist who complies with the request? What demands are placed on the therapist who does not comply, but insists upon conducting treatment in a professionally ethical manner? For further discussion, we refer the interested reader to the chapters on working with parents, transference and countertransference, and pitfalls.

Further, if intensive treatment is most efficacious therapeutically, what of the pressure on therapists, by insurers, to "work faster," decrease frequency of psychotherapy or increase medication dosages? At times, countertransference factors shape the ethical behavior of the therapist in these dilemmas.

While child therapists frequently seek consultation once a serious problem has been identified, it is our position that much of this could be prevented if courses in ethics could illuminate potential difficulties in advance. So we consider this effort to examine ethical practice in treatment of children an integral part of the education of all who engage in child psychotherapeutic work: teachers, supervisors, residents, psychology interns, and social work students.

Lest one glean the impression that our focus is exclusively upon behavior, let us clarify. We are aware that communications between therapist, child and adolescent patients, and parents are governed, in part, by processes both conscious and unconscious. Transference and countertransference (both unconscious processes) are experienced and expressed, continually, in the treatment situation. Unconscious processes of both therapist and patient or parent unavoidably affect the participants in the treatment situation and contribute to the ways thoughts, feelings, and actions take place in the therapeutic relationship.

We hope the reader will find a rich and provocative assembly of useful clinical and theoretical material that will be useful in clinical practice and teaching. While the introduction abounds with questions, we propose to offer ways of thinking about this material in a manner that will help the attentive therapist to provide treatment of the highest quality, that is, a clinical practice that is indistinguishable from ethical practice.

ONE

Clinical Models of Child Psychotherapy and Ethical Issues

There are three basic theoretical models for the clinical treatment of children and their families: behavioral/cognitive; systemic or family; and psychodynamic. Within these three broad categories there are variations. This chapter describes the three models, their variations, and the rationale for employing one clinical approach in favor of another. As models, none is more vulnerable than another to ethical lapses. In the treatment of children, however, there are two over arching principles that influence any model of treatment: development and transference/countertransference. This chapter explores these two fundamental principles and the ways in which a particular clinical model recognizes or fails to recognize their importance. It is when either an understanding of development or an appreciation of transference is ignored that any clinical model becomes vulnerable to ethical transgressions.

COGNITIVE/BEHAVIORAL TREATMENT

This approach to treatment is grounded in the principle that the behavioral manifestations of a child's symptom, regardless of their origin, can be treated directly and efficiently using a learning model in which operationalized techniques are used to extinguish the symptom. The therapist works directly with the child to target a particular symptom and teach the child ways in which the symptom can be eliminated. The child may be taught to practice such techniques as visualization, substitution, and thought blocking. The therapist may also work to help the child learn to ignore his anxiety in the service of not relying on the symptom for comfort, but instead substitute other forms of comfort or rewards. Parents may be involved to insure the child practices these techniques at home. This model requires that the child experiences discomfort with the symptom and has a wish to get rid of it. The approach also requires parents who are invested in the treatment and organized enough to monitor the child's "homework." The basic approach of cognitive/behavioral therapy does not vary according to the developmental level of the child. This approach also does not recognize transference/countertransference dynamics as the emphasis is on consciousness, learning, and cognition.

When cognitive/behavioral therapy is used to target specific discrete symptoms such as phobias, compulsive actions, or obsessive thoughts it can be effective in eliminating the particular symptom. It does not attempt to address whatever underlying issues may have contributed to the creation of the symptom. It can be helpful, however, in giving the patient a way to manage or control a distressing symptom and that may alleviate some of the child's anxiety. In addition, since the child no longer feels driven by the intrusive symptom, he or she may indeed feel more comfortable in participating in social activities and have more psychic energy available for academic work. Feeling free of his symptom and more like his peers and doing better in school may then have a positive impact on the child's self-esteem, which in turn may help the child to move forward developmentally. For some parents, the recognition that their child is able to eliminate his symptom with specific strategies may help them change their view of the child, no longer seeing him as "crazy," obstreperous, or in need of their constant behavioral supervision. In other words, when cognitive/behavioral therapy works, there may be many secondary gains that encourage progressive development and more appropriate parenting.

SYSTEMIC FAMILY THERAPY

This approach emphasizes that the child's difficulties originate in a family "system" and it is this structure that must be altered in order for the child's behavior to change. Usually all members of the family are seen together and the therapist observes and comments on patterns of family behavior, which are thought to be maladaptive and promote the child's difficulties. The model assumes that as family members begin to recognize their maladaptive patterns they will wish to change them. The therapist may be quite direct in offering alternative ways of interacting. This model does appreciate developmental principles, not only as they apply to individuals but also in terms of the evolution of family structures. Developmental child guidance may be offered by the therapist to the parents when it appears some of the family's difficulties stem from a lack of understanding of the developmental level of the child or children. There is, however, no recognition in the model that the child's developmental level may have a significant impact on the therapy itself. Transference and countertransference dynamics are not seen as relevant to this model, since the emphasis is on structural, not unconscious, dynamics.

Family therapy can be quite helpful when the child's symptoms have either developed in response to difficulties within the family or are exacerbated by the family's response to the child. If the symptoms are caused or exacerbated by maladaptive behaviors within the family, as the family changes its patterns of interacting as well as the ways it responds to the symptomatic behavior of the child, the disruptiveness of the behavioral problems should diminish or disappear. If, however, the origin of the child's difficulties has an intrapsychic source, the problems may be reduced, but are unlikely to disappear. Under these circumstances, the parents' new, more adaptive responses to their child's behavior may help reduce the general level of distress within the family, but the child's symptoms will not be eliminated.

PSYCHODYNAMIC THERAPY

There are many types of psychodynamic treatment, including but not limited to psychoanalysis, developmental child guidance, and corrective object relations. All of these approaches have been influenced by fundamental psychoanalytic principles, among them the presence of unconscious as well as conscious mental states; the conviction that behavior stems from unconscious as well as conscious sources; that symptoms represent a "compromise formation" between conflicting forces, both external and internal; that the mind develops in the context of a relationship between infant and mother. These approaches recognize the child's development is shaped by his constitution as well as by his environment; that is, both nature and nurture are understood as equally important. Constitutional forces include both innate capacities with which the child is born as well as age typical fantasies, wishes, and fears that are a part of being human. Environmental factors include parents and siblings, the extended family, cultural influences, as well as socioeconomic forces. Usually the child is the principal patient in the therapy, but developmental guidance may be offered to the parents as well. The importance of the developmental level of the child is recognized as critical and treatment techniques are formulated in terms of the child's developmental level. The importance of both transference and countertransference is recognized. In some approaches, countertransference may be seen as an important source of information about the child patient.

Psychodynamic intervention is based on the notion that symptoms and problematic behavior that have not yielded to time or changes in the external world derive from a complex matrix of constitutional, developmental, and environmental factors that find representation in children's fantasies and theories about themselves, their expectations of the world, and their adaptation to it. In this context, symptoms are seen as a result of children's best efforts both to resolve and to express in disguised form solutions to conflicts among their wishes, the demands of external reality, and developmental capacities. What distinguishes a psychodynamically oriented intervention from other types of clinical intervention is the therapist's conviction that children's behavioral difficulties have as their source the complex interplay between the wishes and fears inherent to children's inner world, their maturational capacities, the pressures of progressive development, and the demands of external reality. Psychodynamic interventions may be employed in a broad range of contexts, including intensive psychotherapy with several sessions per week over a long period of time, weekly psychotherapy, brief psychotherapy, structured sessions, and parent-child guidance. The *guiding principle* of psychodynamic intervention is that throughout development, there is a complex interaction between internal and external demands and children's unfolding capacities to meet these demands. The *goal* of psychodynamic psychotherapy is to help children find alternative solutions to conflicts that give rise to symptoms that interfere with current functioning and progressive development.

Whatever the underlying cause, academic difficulties, constant fights with peers, siblings, and parents, soiling, enuresis, disturbed sleep and eating, social isolation, drug and alcohol abuse, avoidant behavior and phobias, and depressive withdrawal may cause a great deal of discomfort to patients and families. However, seen from a psychodynamic perspective, each of these symptomatic difficulties represents an individual's attempt both to defend against wishes and urges that are experienced as unacceptable and dangerous and to give expression to them in a disguised form. Where symptomatic behavior and age-inappropriate functioning serve children as the best available means of representing internal distress, these symptoms can be viewed as highly condensed modes of communication that no one—not parents, teachers, or patients—has been able to translate fully and understand. Simply put, the aim of psychodynamic psychotherapy is to provide a setting in which patients can increasingly experience safety in exploring previously "unknowable" aspects of their inner world that give rise to conflict, defense, and maladaptive ways in which they negotiate daily life.

From a psychodynamic perspective, difficulties that bring children into treatment represent attempts to avoid or modulate the experience of internal conflict or threats to their sense of well-being. Although it is common to attribute loss of self-esteem to failures in external reality, it is equally possible that the threat to self-esteem stems from internalized conflicts involving the guilt and shame associated with internal moral judgment.

Finding alternative forms of expression and alleviating the necessity of adhering to current modes of response requires the development of a new setting, a new relationship, and a new language in which the dynamic interaction between what is internal and what is experienced in daily life can be explored. Over time, psychotherapy sessions provide a setting in which the child and a relatively neutral adult can examine the themes and consistent patterns of play, discussion, modes of expression, and interpersonal interactions. The clinician's goal is to understand children's internal life, to relate this to their behavior inside and outside of the therapeutic situation, and to try to alter inner or outer functioning through helping children to become better and more understanding observers of their experiences, feelings, thoughts, and life. The psychotherapeutic intervention provides a stage on which, over time, the language of the unconscious—fantasies, conflicts, defenses, and symptoms—can be played out imaginatively, in games and through discussion, thereby becoming observable and translatable, and gradually understood. As the child develops a better understanding of his internal conflicts, these conflicts exert less pressure for expression through the development of symptoms, and the child is able to develop more age-appropriate and adaptive capacities for managing internal conflict. As his behavior becomes more age appropriate, and if the parents become better able to understand the meanings behind the child's symptomatic behaviors, the child's contribution to distress and unhappiness within the family should diminish, allowing the other members of the family to move forward developmentally as well.

THE PRINCIPLE OF DEVELOPMENT

Development is understood as being complex, involving both regressive and progressive forces. It is epigenetic with ever increasing complexity, consolidation, and integration. Development is seen as involving particular psychological tasks at particular points; these tasks are to some extent coordinated with chronological epics. Some developmental models assume the principle of "critical periods," that is if a particular psychological task is not achieved within a certain period it can never be fully achieved. There are multiple "lines" of development that are not necessarily coordinated so that some developmental disharmony is inevitable. It is understood the developmental organization of a child has a direct impact on the approach to psychotherapy and the degree to which the child can appreciate he is the cause of his own suffering; that is, the degree to which the child can appreciate he is the "target" of the treatment depends on where he is developmentally. Not all treatment techniques take the developmental level of the child into account. The appreciation of a therapist for the child's developmental level may have a substantive impact upon the treatment outcome.

It is understood that the developmental organization of the child may be quite different from his chronological age. An approach that may be appropriate for a child at one developmental level will not be so at another.

At each phase of development there tend to be nodal conflicts that inevitably give rise to crises and symptoms of childhood, which evoke concern in the adults who are most involved with children. While the tantrums, separation anxiety, and difficulties in sleeping and eating typical in toddlerhood are troublesome to caregivers, they do not necessarily indicate deviation from normal trends in development. These developmentally expectable symptoms are especially salient during the time of children's emerging recognition that they are individuals, separate and different from their parents, whom the children wish to please in their expectations of more mature behavior. Similarly, the nighttime fears, transient phobias, and defiance of four- to six-year-old children do not automatically represent psychopathology, but rather reflect their active attempts to negotiate conflicts between normal feelings of love, hate, jealousy, and competition. Senior preschoolers or early grade school children have ambivalent feelings about establishing a greater sense of autonomy. These mixed feelings may be expressed in testing rules, tattling on others, social difficulties, rapid shifts in mood, or heightened concerns about bodily changes; they do not automatically signal the need for clinical intervention. Additionally, above and beyond the symptomatology of normal development, children's behavior or mood may change in direct response to clear external precipitants, such as moving to a new house, changing schools, parental discord and divorce, acute illness, exposure to exceptional, traumatic incidents, or it may reflect the stress of coping with cognitively based learning difficulties.

The concept of developmental lines proposes myriad lines of development from an infantile starting point to a mature end point: the development of play, the ability to work, and the child's gender, sexuality, and morality all have a developmental trajectory beginning in early childhood. These lines may have some correlation with chronological age, but they do not necessarily. Development can proceed at a different pace along different lines accounting for the sorts of developmental disharmonies observable in growing up.

The developmental organization of a child influences not only the sort of symptoms that may arise, but how the child makes use of clinical interventions. The toddler or preschool child may suffer from their symptoms, but their experience is that the problem is coming from outside. The young child believes that if only the environment, in the form of parents and siblings, would adapt to his needs, he would experience no difficulty. Although older children and adolescents are somewhat better able to understand that they bear some responsibility for their difficulties, they continue to some extent to experience the cause of their problems as being outside the self. The clinician must determine whether environmental change is indeed the most important factor or whether the child needs to be engaged in recognizing his contribution to his difficulties. If development is taken into account, this assessment of the relative contributions of internal conflict and failures in the environment to the child's difficulties is critical in determining the treatment approach. Although offering inappropriate treatment because the clinician has not taken development into account is not necessarily an ethical problem, it certainly compromises the outcome of any intervention. Without an understanding of development, however, the therapist's handling of gifts, both giving and receiving, gratification in other forms, confidentiality, and privacy may all become ethically compromised.

TRANSFERENCE/COUNTERTRANSFERENCE

Transference is a concept that originated in psychoanalysis and emphasizes that any relationship is influenced unconsciously by past relationships with significant others, primarily parents and siblings. In psychodynamic psychotherapy, it is understood that transference significantly influences the ways the patient experiences the relationship with the therapist. Countertransference is the parallel process in the therapist involving the transference of the therapist to the patient. In some psychodynamic models of treatment, countertransference is believed to be another source of information the therapist has available about what the patient is trying to communicate during a clinical hour. Not sufficiently recognized in many psychodynamic therapies with children is the fact that the child's parents will also have transferences towards the child's therapist and that the therapist will experience countertransference towards the parents.

Transference is the term used to describe or characterize a patient's attitude toward the therapist. The term derives from psychoanalytic treatment with adults and refers to the ways in which patient's perceptions of and relationships with significant figures from childhood are expressed in current perceptions, thoughts, fantasies, feelings, attitudes, and behavior in current relationships. In the clinical situation, transference refers specifically to the ways in which these experiences from the past are organized around and expressed within the relationship with the therapist (Sandler et al., 1980). A major difference in considering this phenomenon in work with children lies in the fact that, unlike adults, children continue to live with and rely on parents. Much of what children bring to the treatment situation reflects not only a transference of aspects of relationships from the past, but significant aspects of current experiences, fantasies, perceptions, feelings, and attitudes from current relationships, particularly those with parents and other family members (Sandler et al., 1980).

In an attempt to clarify the phenomena of transference, particularly as it is observed in the treatment of children, Anna Freud and her colleagues developed a topology of transference: (1) habitual modes of relating, (2) current relationships, (3) past experiences, and (4) transference neurosis (Sandler et al., 1980). The first type refers to fixed ways of relating to others that, while deriving from earlier relationships, have now been applied to the world at large or to whole categories of people with whom children have contact. The second category refers to the transfer or displacement of current preoccupations with real situations in children's lives or with aspects of current developmental challenges. The emphasis here is on the distinction between a revival of past experiences versus the displacement of current ones, which can be observed in children's relationships with the analyst. The third category involves children's attitudes, fantasies, and memories from the past, which were previously repressed and are now manifested in the current relationship with the therapist as it develops during regular contact over a sustained period of time. In child psychotherapy, it is much less common to see as much evidence of the transference neurosis as occurs in the analysis and psychotherapy of adults. When it emerges, there is a significant shift in the patient's attention, interests, and preoccupations to a focus on the interaction with the therapist.

The notion that children's attitudes to the therapist tell us something about their internal frame of reference or internal configurations of experience, urges, feelings, and fantasies would seem to suggest the encounter with the new person—the therapist—is mainly a reflection of children's lives outside the consulting room. This notion assumes the therapist's presentation and modes of relating to children have no or only minimal bearing on the ways the children present themselves in this particular setting. The opposite view suggests the therapist's demeanor and the particular circumstances of the encounter have everything to do with children's presentation and therefore skew the nature and significance of their attitude to the clinician as a prominent source of data or window into their inner world. These two views reflect the extremes in considering the extent to which children's manifest attitudes toward the therapist are a pure reflection of their inner life or of their day-to-day experiences outside of the consulting room. That is, children's attitudes in isolation from other aspects of the fuller presentation of themes and emotional presentation may, in fact, tell the therapist very little about the children's central interests, fantasies, concerns, and modes of regulating and communicating them. In addition, even when considering children's attitudes in the broader context, initial impressions may not be borne out as the fuller picture of the children emerges over the course of the psychotherapy treatment.

Rapid shifts in children's presentation may occur, from friendly, positive engagement to attitudes of hostility, disappointment, and fear. It is important to remember that children's attitudes to the therapist develop in the context of a unique setting and special relationship.

Less well recognized are the transferences parents experience in their relationship with their child's therapist. Expectations about what treatment can do are influenced not only by the therapist's presentation and experience, but by the parents' experiences with figures from their past: their own parents, teachers, physicians, and others from whom the parents hoped for help. Parental transferences can manifest themselves in enumerable ways: in parental doubt about the efficacy of the treatment or the skill of the therapist, in the expectation that the therapist can change the child into the child the parents always wished for, and in feelings of resentment at being excluded from the child's treatment as the therapist protects the child's privacy and confidentiality.

The therapist also develops transferences to the child and the parents. This sort of transference is referred to as "countertransference," a concept that originated in the notion that the therapist would have an unconsciously driven response to the patient's transference. Failure to recognize countertransference on the part of the therapist can result in ethical lapses. Typical countertransference fantasies that when unrecognized can prove dangerous, are: the belief that one is a better parent to the child patient than the parents are; the wish to "rescue" the child through treatment; a fantasy of omnipotence in which only this particular therapist is skilled enough to treat this child and all the family members; a conviction that if the therapist's interventions are well meant, any intervention will be helpful. Countertransferences such as these can lead a therapist to violate boundaries between family members, to forget the necessity of privacy and confidentiality, and to give authoritative advice based on nothing more than the therapist's own cultural expectations.

CONCLUSION

Although the three basic models of therapy for children: cognitive, family, and psychodynamic, do not lead to interventions that are likely to cause ethical problems, failure to recognize the critical importance of development and transference/countertransference may lead to ethical violations.

REFERENCES

Freud, A. 1965. *The writings of anna freud*, (Vol. 6). Madison, CT: International University Press, Inc.

Sandler, J., Kennedy, H., & Tyson, R. (1980). *Technique of child psychoanalysis: Discussions with anna freud*. Cambridge, MA: Harvard University Press.

TWO

Ethical Dilemmas Shaped by Transference and Countertransference

Transference and countertransference have been defined and described in the chapter on clinical models. In this chapter, we address specific ways these unconscious processes can affect the course of treatment with respect to the interplay of unconscious communication between child therapist and child patient. It is this interchange, when related to conflict of which one is unaware that may lead to ethical lapses and/or boundary violations.

Several categories of potential difficulties will be addressed. First, in the case of a therapist who wishes, unconsciously, to please (or displease) his or her patient, and a young patient who has similar impulses toward the therapist, assiduous work is required for the therapist to become aware of unconscious transference and countertransference impulses toward the child patient. It is the unconscious aspects of these wishes and impulses that may lead to ethical problems.

As the child or adolescent patient regresses during the treatment, in the context of transference, the therapist may experience substantive unconscious pressure to regress as well. It is an awareness of such potential that serves to protect the therapist from ethical lapses.

The child therapist may experience both pressure to regress and pressure to act in a manner that is different from work with adult patients. As the child patient expresses conflicts in action rather than in words, the child therapist who is less aware of unconscious phenomena may experience impulses to respond in action as well. When the therapist responds to the child patient with regression (sleepiness, for example) and action (instead of language), this may intrude upon the therapeutic space and provide an avenue for ethical problems.

For the child patient, the therapist, in the transference, may unconsciously represent the parent of the past (very early childhood) or the parent of the present. The therapist may also represent a sibling or other significant person in the child's life. The same is true for the therapist, who may view the child patient through the prism of her/his own early childhood. For example, a therapist who treats a child who enjoys competitive games may become competitive with the child, losing perspective of his or her task as an adult professional who is responsible for a child's treatment. With self-reflection, the therapist may become aware that the child patient reminds him of a sibling from his early childhood, with whom he or she competed ferociously. Lack of awareness of this potential for unconscious responses may lead to a treatment that is focused upon "winning" a game rather than providing an environment for a child to resolve conflicts and progress developmentally.

The child or adolescent in treatment may idealize the therapist and wish, at times, the therapist were his or her parent. Ethical problems arise when the therapist is unaware of his or her own wish to serve as the child's parent. This may take the form of subtly seductive behavior, inappropriate gifts, and encouraging the child to "keep secrets" from the parents, undermining the efforts of the parents on the child's behalf. Such behavior leads to ethical misconduct. The therapist's full awareness of impulses and ability to think about conflicts in this area is another area for preventive work, thus ensuring a treatment of high ethical standards.

A good deal of attention is given to working with the child or adolescent's aggressive impulses toward the therapist. It is the child's libidinal impulses that can lead to ethical issues, particularly when the therapist is not fully aware of what impulses are evoked in him or her. When the three year old dives into the analyst's lap, he or she anticipates a safe environment, and it is most common that the patient will be gently set down and the two may deal with this, either directly or by displacement in the context of play. When an early adolescent girl attempts to disrobe or to "show" her "new underwear" to her therapist, the therapist must be aware of his or her libidinal impulses in order to intervene in a manner that is effective, therapeutic, and respectful. Once again, it is the lack of awareness of libidinal impulses that leads to "acting-out," which endangers the child's treatment.

Lest the reader imagine that all that is necessary is "awareness," we emphasize more is involved. Even the "aware" therapist may yield to libidinal and aggressive impulses, in the context of transferences and countertransferences to the child. The impulse to act may be conscious. The wish to permit the child to exhibit her or his body may overwhelm the knowledge of ethical guidelines. Matters of conscience are surely in the realm, at least in part, of that which is conscious. A risk to ethical practice takes place when the therapist begins to dismiss his or her own perspective of what is ethical and react only to that which provides personal gratification. In these cases, the therapist may rationalize his or her behavior by considering it, for example, a "corrective emotional experience." Such transgressions are more likely to take place in the case of illness of the therapist, profound personal conflicts, external stress, and fantasies of omniscience and omnipotence that take precedence over reality. Conscience supports ethical behavior. When the conscience is anchored in an obsessional structure, or is excessively harsh for a wide variety of reasons, the ability of the therapist to perform in an ethical manner may be compromised. So we expand our notion of a workable conscience to one that is both firmly rooted and appropriately flexible. Therapeutic work with children requires a high degree of self-observation, and also requires a conscience that is in excellent working order. All patients are vulnerable in the context of their transferences. Children and adolescents are even more susceptible to a therapist whose conscience is not structurally sound.

Another element that increases risk of ethical lapses in the context of transference is when the therapist treats a child whom he or she idealizes. For example, if the child is a "star" in sports or art or some area of special interest and the therapist, as a child, always longed to hold such a position but was unable to achieve this, the therapist may unconsciously identify with the child and lose sight of his or her task of helping the patient with his or her internal suffering. At every juncture of the therapist's making an intervention, there is both a therapeutic choice and an ethical decision. Intervening in the best mode clinically is also acting upon that which is ethical. Ideally, the two are fully integrated.

Another area for lapse takes place when the therapist withdraws from the patient by becoming distracted or sleepy. A young male child therapist felt bored by his eight-year-old patient and began to fall asleep, momentarily, during the late afternoon sessions, when the patient insisted upon playing board games. When the therapist began to reflect upon his behavior, which he found distressing, he realized when he was the same age as his patient he played only sports and imagined that board games "were for sissies." He had repressed this thought for decades. As he regressed in treating his young patient, his early idea of "board games are for sissies" re-emerged, although it was not fully conscious. In fighting off the "sissy" impulse, the therapist began to actually fall asleep as the patient engaged in play. When the therapist recognized the impulses he feared as an eight-year-old, and even to some degree in the present, he was able to treat his young patient in an alert, fully conscious, and therapeutic manner.

The essential piece, in the context of ethical dilemmas of transference and countertransference, is that two main factors are present in preventing unnecessary interference to the treatment of children. First, the therapist must be alert to his or her feelings and impulses toward the child patient, able to analyze them, and willing to seek consultation when difficulties arise. Second, the therapist must be aware of impulses to dismiss matters of conscience in favor of fantasies of immediate gratification and to seek consultation when such matters present themselves.

The conscience of the child and adolescent patient is still in the process of development. A therapist represents, for the child patient, both a transference object and a developmental object. Psychotherapeutic work with children requires a therapist whose maturity and ethical principles are based upon a firm foundation so that the child or adolescent can resolve conflicts and proceed developmentally.

THREE

Ethical Considerations in Our Work with Parents

Working with the parents of our child and adolescent patients is one of the essential and challenging tasks of our work as child and adolescent therapists. Our work with parents presents unique ethical issues, dilemmas, and questions that do not arise in our work with adult patients. Central to these issues is when the therapist works with adult patients, the patient-therapist dyad is the primary focus, but when treating children and adolescents the therapist must necessarily include work with parents and other significant adults in the child and adolescent's life. In addition, the young child and the adolescent are directly vulnerable to the decisions made by their parents and by the therapist as well. Complicated and perplexing ethical issues arise in each aspect of our work with children, adolescents, and parents. The ethical principles, which guide our conduct as therapists, include issues of boundaries, diagnoses, forms of treatment, decisions about medication, and encompass broader ethical questions that arise during treatment. This chapter sets forth the ethical issues, questions, and dilemmas which every therapist faces and it offers approaches and guidelines to help inform the choices and decisions we make in our daily therapeutic work. We will also focus on the positive clinical effects of practicing within a clear ethical framework. Multiple transferences in child cases, as well as complex countertransference issues, will be addressed because these matters are pivotal in thinking about ethical issues and practice in work with children and adolescents.

There is no one right way to work with parents in the context of engaging therapeutically with their children, although there are ethical and technical principles that offer us grounding. Each family presents with individual and unique strengths and difficulties so that within a broad ethical frame the therapist must consider thoughtful application of specific principles to clinical issues and clinical moments.

The tasks of working with parents who ask for a consultation about a troubled child or adolescent include gathering information about the child or adolescent's early history, precipitating issues in the current consultation and, as part of this process, helping the parents understand their child and the meaning of his or her behavior and symptoms. The therapist also learns the family history of both parents which helps to establish rapport with the parents as well as reach a deeper understanding of their child or adolescent. The therapist also assists the parents in developing conviction about the desirability and need for treatment. He or she also establishes and maintains a mutual working alliance with the parents for the treatment to take place and to strengthen the parent-child relationship as part of the treatment process. Ethical decisions often involve reconciling potentially conflicting goals such as preserving the child and adolescent's confidential material while helping the parents understand their child and his or her need for treatment.

We suggest some central questions for the therapist to ask him or herself. Is the child or adolescent aware of our meetings with his or her parents? How are we thinking about this issue? How does the work with the parents affect the child or adolescent? Will the therapist's relationship with the parents heighten loyalty conflicts for the child or adolescent patient? What kind of work with the parents is genuinely in the best interest of the child? How will the work with the parents affect the transferences of the child to the therapist which develop during treatment? What is the nature of the transference-countertransference of the therapist to the child patient and to his or her family? How will the work with the parents affect the progressive development of their child? How will the work with the parents help the parent-child relationship develop? What form of parent guidance is most helpful to the parents who want to change their relationship with their child? These are questions that every therapist considers within the ethical frame of practice. What is the role of ethics in these questions? The therapist must be available to parents in order to help them understand what their child is struggling with, yet he or she must preserve confidentiality for the child and adolescent. The therapist must make decisions of diagnosis and treatment that are based upon sound clinical judgment, and not upon simply providing parents that which they imagine and hope would be most desirable for their child.

Understanding the rationale and the aims of different approaches to parent work is central to the therapist's making effective choices in the conduct of the parent work. The therapist is most effective when he or she has a conscious understanding of what is mutative in his or her approach. For example, is it insight, is it a corrective emotional experience, or is it the interpersonal relationship? These theoretical emphases affect how the parent work is focused and structured and how the therapist selects his or her clinical interventions. Misunderstanding these therapeutic modalities can be confusing to the therapist and blur the boundaries of treatment. One example is of a therapist assuming the role of a "friend" of the family in the course of the treatment of their child or adolescent. This behavior might be rationalized by the therapist as facilitating the child, adolescent, and parents' development, but it is usually not helpful to the parents or the child or adolescent's therapeutic work.

> How do we as therapists develop our own professional ethical framework and stance with our patients? Clearly we must start with a foundation of personal integrity which is shaped by our professional training and experience. Developing self-awareness of our vulnerabilities through self-examination and personal psychological treatment allows us to monitor the objectivity of our decision-making. Continuing consultation with experienced colleagues is essential to examining and maintaining our ethical stance as we confront complex ethical issues in our psychotherapeutic work. In this way, the therapist develops a professional ethical ego ideal, which serves to protect the practitioner from ethical lapses. (Ascherman and Rubin, p. 1).

The therapist is guided by a conscious stable ethical framework when he or she is facing the complexities of working with the parents of his or her child and adolescent patients. A major focus of the therapist's work with parents is to help the parents understand their child or adolescent's behavior, fears, and symptoms with a fresh perspective and renewed energy for investing in the child's treatment and for facing difficult times. To accomplish this, the therapist must be able to put him or herself "into the shoes" of all family members to understand the parental perspective: their concerns, guilt, anger, and fears about their child or adolescent as well as their own involvement in their child's difficulties. It is important to learn about the parents' deepest fears and wishes for their child, and to understand what took place in the childhoods of each parent, particularly at the age their child is currently, at the time they are requesting treatment. Most poignant are the feelings of failure felt by many parents who seek treatment for their child. Parents fear they will be replaced by the therapist in their child's affections and that the therapist may seem to be a better parent than they in the eyes of their child. The therapist, to be effective, makes transitory identifications not only with his or her patient, but with the parents and other significant people in the child and adolescent's life as well. This enables the therapist to understand the clinical situation from multiple points of view and to identify the most effective modes of therapeutic intervention. The therapist's firm grounding in his or her ethical framework enables the therapist to maintain an ethical stance amid often conflicting pressures in the clinical situation.

Mr. and Mrs. "S" came to the therapist to consult about their adolescent daughter whom they felt was "bad" and immoral due to her habitual lying and stealing. They were very troubled, felt guilty, angry, and helpless. They blamed their daughter and alternately tried to control her and turned away from her. They appeared to be giving up. During a period of treatment, the therapist was able to help these parents understand the meanings underlying these behaviors and move away from judging and blaming their daughter so they could address more effectively the issues underlying this self-destructive behavior. These parents initially insisted that the therapist stop the behavior and intervene in an authoritarian manner in their daughter's life. They threatened to interrupt the treatment if the problems did not disappear quickly. With continuing work with these parents, the therapist was able to help them bear their daughter's difficult behavior and understand what lay behind it without betraying the confidentiality of her patient. The therapist's balanced stance toward the patient and her parents initially appeared permissive to Mr. and Mrs. "S." It was crucial to the success of the therapy that the therapist, working in a sustained and patient manner within an ethical frame, was able to help these parents understand the therapeutic reasons for this nonjudgmental and seemingly permissive approach.

Therapists confront a central ethical issue as they work with parents to understand why their children and adolescents feel and behave as they do. The therapeutic space for the child and adolescent needs to be protected, but parents also need to feel they are included and essential to the success of the treatment.

Parents want to know what is happening in the office with their child and what is being treated—in other words, what is the goal of the treatment and how will that goal be reached? They also worry about what the child is not saying and may want to offer frequent "progress reports" to "move things along." Parents are interested in progress and improvement and they will withstand the difficulties of the treatment if they feel that their child is "getting better" and they are an important part of making this progress happen.

The ethical question is, "What do we tell the parents about our work with the child and how do we do this without breaching confidentiality?" There is a range of theoretical perspectives among therapists, particularly with respect to their sharing the child's privileged communication with his or her parents. From one perspective, therapists feel they can't say anything to parents about their work with their child or adolescent patient. These therapists take the position that risking the loss of the child's trust, especially when parents repeat what they have learned at home, may destroy the child's trust not only in the current therapist but in future ones as well. From a different point of view, some therapists share more detailed information about the child or adolescent with the parents believing this to be helpful, which may lead the child or adolescent patient to mistrust the therapist. Parents also may feel overloaded if the therapist gives too much information, especially if it offered in an overly intellectual or abstract manner. Once the child's trust is broken, it may not be possible to restore it, perhaps even in subsequent efforts at treatment.

Some parents are very insistent about knowing the specifics and details of what is taking place in the child's play and behaviors especially when the child frequently runs out of the office to the waiting room or resists coming to his or her session, seemingly, to the parent, avoiding the therapy. This is also true when an adolescent is engaged in self-destructive behavior because parents feel anxious, often angry, and helpless to change this "acting out." Parents feel alarmed when their adolescent is anorexic or bulimic, is cutting herself, or is using drugs and is sexually promiscuous. Parents' request for details may also take place in the absence of difficult behaviors in the child and adolescent, as the parents experience anxiety, fears, and shifting feelings toward the therapist as the child or adolescent's treatment progresses with its inevitable troubled periods. It is often helpful to discuss at the start of the therapy what the parents may expect to experience during the course of the therapy. It is especially important to help the parents understand that when their child or adolescent seems to be getting worse, sometimes this means he or she may actually be getting better. In periods of heightened anxiety or when the child temporarily distances him or herself from the parents, the therapist needs to pay particular attention to the parents' fear of being "left out" and disregarded.

The ethical stance guiding how to explain the child or adolescent's issues to his or her parents while protecting the child or adolescent's clinical material emphasizes the principle of confidentiality of the child and adolescent's material. Therapists can become comfortable with explaining the conflicts the child or adolescent is struggling with, the sources of the troubling behaviors, and the defenses the child relies on in descriptive terms without giving information about the specific content of the treatment sessions. Each therapist must find the most compatible way for him or her to discuss their child or adolescent patient with his or her parents while protecting the privileged communications of the child or adolescent.

The therapist might say that twelve-year-old Johnny is pushing his parents away and behaves in a surly manner at times as his way of trying to feel more independent. Susie is struggling with worries and fears, which makes her socially reticent and interferes with her doing her best at school. The therapist is describing the patient's conflicts, feelings, and defenses in general and using descriptive language without revealing the content of the therapy sessions. Helping parents to understand the current problems of their child or adolescent in the context of what they have observed in their child's earlier development, can often help the parents discover for themselves what is happening in the present within the perspective of the past.

If parents are insistent on knowing more about the sessions, as often occurs when there is school failure, drug and alcohol use, dangerous sexual behavior, suicidal thoughts, and other serious issues and behavior, the therapist must work with these parent to understand their anxiety, anger, guilt, and pain that may lie behind this pressure. Acknowledging the parents realistic worry is essential. Of paramount importance is the therapist's capacity to recognize when their patient is in serious difficulty that requires direct interventions to protect the patient from self-harm. Part of setting the frame of the treatment at the start of the work is to be clear with the patient and his or her parents at what points it would be necessary for the therapist to discuss the patient's behavior directly with his or her parents. If this becomes necessary, the therapist has a basis of understanding with the patient and the parents that protection of the child or adolescent's well-being takes precedence over the principle of confidentiality.

Often, education about how therapy works is helpful to parents who doubt the usefulness of psychotherapy. Parents can usually learn to understand the reasons why confidentiality is important to the success of the treatment. Ascherman and Rubin have found, "The challenge faced in balancing a child's need for reasonable privacy against the parents' need for reasonable information can be shared candidly with parents or guardians" (p. 8). Many parents speak of being curious about what their child talks about and does in his or her therapy, but they are able to learn to restrain themselves from asking their child, respecting his or her privacy. A further goal is to help the parents move from the first step of restraint to acceptance of the child's treatment as belonging to the child within a protected space. Parents who cannot take this step frequently communicate indirectly their strong wish to learn what goes on in the therapy sessions, which interferes with the child's capacity to use his or her therapy freely.

The course of this young adult's therapy illustrates this issue. When she was an eighteen-year-old freshman in college, she became severely depressed. Her anxious parents requested a consultation with the therapist who recommended she see a psychiatrist in the city where she was attending college. As a young adult she transferred to a local college and saw the therapist, who had met with her parents previously, with whom she began psychotherapy. After a period of twice-weekly psychotherapy, now a young adult, she entered into an analysis that lasted for five years. Her parents divorced while she was in treatment; she felt caught in a conflict of loyalties between her parents. At this time, as she was terminating her analysis, her mother experienced her daughter becoming aloof and distant with her, which she attributed to the negative influence of the therapist on her daughter. The mother requested an appointment to talk with the therapist expecting he would schedule an appointment with her as he had in their previous consultation.

Her daughter made it clear she did not want the therapist to talk with her mother and she would let her mother know of her decision. The mother responded to her daughter's decision by entering a complaint with this therapist's colleagues, protesting that the therapist was unduly influencing her daughter against her. This mother was told that in analytic and psychotherapeutic treatment, maintaining the confidentiality of the patient is crucial to the success of the treatment. It was also explained to the mother that when the therapist first met with her, her daughter was an adolescent; parents are often involved in their child's treatment during the adolescent period but this may change in young adulthood.

The interventions of the mother had repercussions in the treatment. The termination phase of the analysis was accelerated and incomplete due to the effect of the mother's influence on both the patient and the therapist. The therapist had felt that his patient's desire that the therapist not talk with her mother was an expression of the gains toward individuation that she had made in her analysis. However, the mother's intervention reawakened her earlier conflicts about her mother. The therapist's ethical stance was affected as he felt caught up in a conflict between pursuing the treatment to completion or hastening the working through of the termination phase. In addition, the therapist felt the threat of potential judgment by his peers even though no fault was found, but this aroused early, buried fears in the therapist, which affected his work with his patient. Would it have been appropriate for the therapist to send a note to this mother explaining that he could not speak with her now without her adult daughter's permission? The patient would need to give permission to the therapist to send such a note, but would the therapist's doing so have interfered with her new found autonomy?

This clinical situation illustrates how important it is to work with the parents of our patients, especially those in long term therapy, to help them understand the changes that will occur in their relationship with their child and with the therapist as the child progresses through the developmental stages into adolescence and young adulthood.

Parents require help to understand that during the course of therapy, their relationship with the therapist may change as their child or adolescent makes significant progress.The example of this young adult and her mother illustrates the importance of conducting parent work within a clear ethical frame.

Ethical questions arise in situations in which certain parents present the therapist with severe personal conflicts and pathology that are outside the scope of what can typically be addressed during the parental meetings. The conflicts and struggles of these parents have the potential to push the therapist to commit ethical lapses such as breaching confidentiality, inappropriately stepping outside the therapeutic role, or becoming a primary therapist to the parents.

Ethical questions arise in situations in which certain parents present the therapist with severe personal conflicts and pathology that are outside the scope of what can typically be addressed during the parental meetings. The conflicts and struggles of these parents have the potential to push the therapist to commit ethical lapses such as breaching confidentiality, inappropriately stepping outside the therapeutic role, or becoming a primary therapist to the parents.

There is no formula for work with the parents of the children and adolescents we are treating, but there are principles that help us make choices and guide our decisions about technique. Each case presents individual issues and clinical questions. The therapist is guided by the overarching ethical principle of doing what is "in the best interest" of their child and adolescent patients. A useful guideline to help prevent ethical lapses in work with parents is to focus on their capacities to perform as effective parents, which may be compromised by conflict and pathology or, conversely, may be relatively free of interference despite the parents' pathology. Focusing on the immediate conflicts interfering with parenting and supporting parental strengths may protect the therapist from crossing boundaries, breaching confidentiality, or losing his or her ethical stance with the family and the child or adolescent.

The mother of a mid-adolescent girl in treatment with a male therapist did not actively try to sabotage her child's treatment, but she made it clear she would neither function as the "chauffeur" nor pay for the treatment. This did not stop her from actively participating in the parent conferences. She was blatantly seductive towards this male therapist, even inviting him to engage socially on two occasions. In mid-adolescence, her daughter was becoming quite seductive, to some degree an identification with her mother. The therapist thought that as his patient changed, her mother might well experience considerable internal discomfort and interrupt her daughter's treatment. How do we think about working with this mother? Could she respond to an approach that would help her to understand her own behavior and its connection with the behavior of her daughter? If not, how does the analyst/therapist establish firm limits on the mother's behavior toward him in the context of preserving the treatment frame? How does he do this without alienating this mother, a situation that could bring his patient's treatment to a premature end. Could this mother have been helped to focus with the therapist on finding her strengths as a parent so she could feel satisfaction in more appropriately parenting her daughter?

Careful thought needs to be given to an approach that prevents the development of boundary problems in the context of protecting this adolescent's treatment. The therapist must take into account the conflicts and defenses the parent presents, the ways in which these intertwine with the child or adolescent's conflicts and defenses, as well as the vulnerabilities of both the parent and the therapist. Above all, the therapist must maintain clear boundaries between himself and this mother for the treatment to proceed.

The therapist brings a number of issues to his or her work with parents, which may lead to ethical problems. Transferences and countertransferences are a central dynamic in boundary issues arising in work with parents. The therapist's countertransference responses to the parental transferences and to the dynamics and clinical material in work with parents are crucial for the therapist to recognize in himself or herself and to understand. These countertransferences that arise from the therapist's unconscious fantasies, conflicts, and defenses require self-reflection and self-examination as they may impact the treatment. Often outside the therapist's awareness, they have the potential to result in ethical missteps on the part of the therapist. However, not all the therapist's reactions and feelings toward the parents of his or her patients are countertransference. The therapist may feel anger, anxiety, sadness, and other feelings that are appropriate to the material parents bring to the parent work. The therapist is helped to understand the parents and to empathize with them when he or she allows him or herself to experience what the parents are feeling and to be aware of his or her personal reactions to emotionally laden material. Situations involving illness, loss, disappointment, and other affects may touch the therapist deeply. The therapist needs to allow him or herself to experience these feelings while using them in the service of the work with the parents. An ethical choice occurs, not uncommonly, when the parents and the therapist have suffered a similar loss, such as the death of a family member. The therapist may think it would be helpful to the parents to share his or her loss with them and he or she may feel considerable internal pressure to do so. Careful thought is required as the sharing of such a loss, though motivated by empathy, may create a considerable burden for the parents and the parent work.

The various people involved with the child's treatment lead to multiple identifications, transferences, and countertransferences, which become confusing for the therapist who is not aware of the serious potential for problems they pose. This includes not only interactions with parents but teachers, caregivers, grandparents, and other significant figures in the child's life. Ascherman and Rubin pose the challenge that the therapist confronts:

> Protecting the child's privacy can be a complex and difficult challenge as we concurrently work with the parents to learn about their child's development in the context of family dynamics, interface with the schools to evaluate the child's educational strengths and weaknesses and potentially with the justice system and other agencies to advocate for the child's need" (p. 6).

It is important for the therapist to remember that the transferences of the parents and other significant people in the child's life to him or her can influence, in a profound manner, how the parents and others experience what the therapist is saying to them. Conversely, these multiple transferences can profoundly influence the therapist's responses to both the parents of the patient and the patient as well, sometimes leading to acting on unconscious impulses resulting in unexpected boundary crossings and violations.

An ethical framework is especially important to protect the child therapist from the regressive pull when his or her child or adolescent patients regress in their treatment. The child or adolescent's level of development arouses unconscious developmental issues and conflicts from this same developmental period in the therapist's life. The same is true of work with parents. If the parent is troubled by preoedipal pathology, for example, the pressures exerted in the transference may elicit from the therapist his or her own difficulties from early in life. Feelings of envy, jealousy, sibling competition, separation problems, and hurts from narcissistic injury endured in childhood can give rise to common conflicts and feelings experienced by the child and adolescent therapist. When these early conflicts dovetail with that of the parent, the therapist and parent may become locked in an unhelpful difficult position or impasse. For example, the therapist who asserts, "I hate those parents," may not be aware that he or she is reacting to the child patient's parents as if they were the therapist's own parents of early childhood. It is these unconscious phenomena, unrecognized, that can lead to ethical breaches. This is a significant reason for therapists to consult with colleagues about their responses to the parents of their patients. One useful warning sign manifests itself when the therapist finds him or herself behaving in a way that is not usual or customary for him or herself in any particular situation. The therapist needs to think through what is pushing him or her out of his or her customary role, often with help from consultation.

The child and adolescent patient often communicates in his or her therapy through the mode of action leading to pressure on the therapist to regress and to act, which is sometimes carried over into work with the parents. The therapist's issues of early childhood with his or her parents come into play in parent sessions, often unrecognized. Over identification with the child in the therapist's meetings with parents whom the therapist feels are not "good" parents for the child requires careful self-examination of these critical feelings on the part of the therapist. Fantasies of being a better parent to the child require substantive self-reflection. It is wise for the therapist to examine his or her own beliefs about parenting and feelings about his or her performance as a parent, both the "successes" and the "failures," to avoid becoming judgmental in the meetings with the parents. These factors make parent work particularly difficult so that the therapist may be prone to commit, even unconsciously, boundary crossings or violations. We strongly emphasize the need for continuing reflective self-examination in work with parents whose children are in treatment. Frequently, consultation with a colleague is very helpful, even essential, to the therapist who is trying to grasp his or her complex feelings that arise in parent work. A discussion of problematic situations with an objective consultant or supervisor helps prevent ethical missteps and strengthens the ethical stance of the therapist.

Ethical conduct with respect to the roles of the various professional adults involved with the therapist's child or adolescent patients and their families is crucial to the conduct of each case. Each professional's role should be made explicit and the ethical principles regarding confidentiality applied to the relationships between professionals. For example, when the therapist thinks that psychological testing would provide helpful understanding to the work with a child or adolescent, the therapist needs to explore this with the parents, who are often reluctant to undertake this testing. The parents may feel that the testing will make the child feel "different"; and they may be fearful of what the testing might reveal. The therapist needs to work with these concerns, often over time, to help the parents accept the recommendation for testing. Explanation of the reasons for the testing and attention to parental anxieties enable most parents to proceed with the recommendation. The question then arises, "Should the psychological tester or the therapist interpret the test results to the parents and the child or adolescent?" This decision should be based on careful consideration of what is in the best interests of the parents and child in regard to understanding the results of the test. With particularly vulnerable parents, it may be most helpful for the therapist to interpret the test results to the parents in the context of his or her relationship with them and clinical knowledge about their child over time, especially when the testing will be difficult for the parents to hear. In order to avoid misunderstandings between the psychological tester and the therapist, it is important that they clarify their roles with each other in the interests of the specific case under discussion.

In one case of an adolescent whose parents did not fully accept the seriousness of their child's difficulties, the psychological tester and the therapist did not discuss their respective roles and the preparation for how the parents might react to the test results was not sufficient. When the psychologist interpreted the results of the test in a single session with these parents, it proved to be so narcissistically wounding that the parents withdrew their child from treatment with the therapist immediately. Had the therapist interpreted the test in the context of her knowledge of the adolescent and her relationship with the parents, this unfortunate interruption might not have occurred. The failure to consider the respective roles of the therapist and the psychological tester in the light of the dynamics of this case resulted in an interrupted treatment to the detriment of the adolescent.

Setting the frame at the start of the treatment with both the parents and the child or adolescent and discussing expectations for the therapeutic work helps establish the basis for ethical practice throughout the duration of the treatment. Setting the frame includes defining limits and boundaries for the treatment for both the parents and the child or adolescent. The frame includes establishing the frequency of treatment hours and schedule as well as an agreement about fees. The setting of the fee requires a clear discussion with the parents of the child or adolescent about the amount of the fee and the expectations for payment as well as any anticipated changes in circumstances, which would require an adjustment of the fee. The fee that is set should be financially workable for both the family and for the therapist. The therapist must be able to feel comfortable discussing both the realities of and the meaning of the fee with the parents. This includes discussion of the parents' feelings about the fee and the effect of their attitude about it on their child. Children often hear their parents discussing payment for their treatment and will bring this subject into his or her hours with questions or sometimes with concern that the parents are upset about paying the therapist. The therapist needs to discuss these concerns with the child and the effect the parents' feelings are having on him or her. A question frequently arises about whether the parents will send the payment to the therapist or whether the child will give the payment to the therapist in his or her hour. Ethical practice would include consideration of the age and developmental stage of the child as well as what both the child and the parents are comfortable with. The child may have fantasies about the payment such as, if the parents are paying for the treatment does the therapist really care for him or her? The therapist may depart from a therapeutic stance, becoming irritated or anxious, if the child or adolescent continually forgets to bring the payment to him or her.

An ethical problem occurs when a parent refuses to pay at some point during the course of the treatment. In some instances, a parent will refuse further payment for the treatment thus presenting the therapist with a conflict over his or her obligation to the child and the problem of the parent breaking the frame. The therapist feels an obligation to the child and recognizes the potential harm in interrupting the treatment. On the other hand, the therapist, in addition to the practical matter of finances, does not want to set an example for the older child, in particular, to appear to accept the non-payment, which represents a breach of the agreement on the part of the parents. If the parents are adamant about non-payment, but expect the treatment to continue and this cannot be resolved, the therapist has to weigh the effects on the child or adolescent and on himself or herself. Discussion of this issue among therapists reveals how wrenching the decision to terminate the treatment can be. If the therapist decides to suspend the treatment of the child or adolescent, it may help the child or adolescent to be clear that this is the parents' decision and that they are deciding what they think is best. However, it is important that the child or adolescent's perception of the reasons for his or her parents' decision not be denied by the therapist. The therapist must work with the child or adolescent to understand the meaning of the parents' decision to them. Each child or adolescent will have his own understanding of the reasons for the discontinuation of treatment. The therapist needs to take the cues from the patient in regard to his or her perceptions, awareness of the reasons for interruption, and salient conflicts and defenses in deciding how to discuss the termination with each particular patient.

A parent or family undergoing a hardship such as job loss, illness, or other changes in circumstances, but want to continue the treatment for their child or adolescent, present a different situation. The therapist and family might work together to find a solution acceptable to both. Often, with some flexibility on the therapist's part as well as effort by the family, both financial and practical arrangements can be developed that are mutually satisfactory. In some instances, the therapist can reduce the fee or accept delayed payment. The therapist can also offer specific suggestions, helping the family to explore possible options for themselves.

Maintaining the frame throughout the treatment is an important part of the prevention of ethical problems. The frame is a guidepost to help the therapist and parents stay on an ethical course in the face of the inevitable issues that arise in treatment. This is especially true when parents have strong disagreements about undertaking and continuing treatment or one parent refuses to participate, which sometimes occurs when parents are divorced or otherwise in conflict and the child or adolescent becomes the focus of their conflicts. Of course, the therapist would try to work with these situations to help both parents to participate in the best interest of their child but failing success, the therapist will need to decide whether and how to proceed with the participating parent only.

Difficult ethical decisions arise when parents divorce. If divorce appears likely during the initial consultation with parents whose child needs treatment, it is important for the therapist to clarify at that time the limits of his or her role in such a case. When parents are anticipating a divorce, they will often expect the therapist to testify in court, in the divorce proceedings, and in custody disputes. Sometimes parents do not make this expectation explicit at the outset of consulting with the therapist. In most cases, if the therapist of the child takes a position supporting one parent over another in a divorce dispute, the child's treatment is compromised. The therapist must make clear to the parents that he or she will not testify in court and explain to the parents that this would seriously interfere with the therapist's helping their child work through the many conflicting feelings that children and adolescents' have when their parents divorce.

From an ethical perspective, the therapist would recommend the family obtain a psychologist or psychiatrist whose task it is solely to evaluate what is best for the child and offer findings in court.

Ethical issues arise when several colleagues are actively involved in the same case. For example, questions frequently arise over whether, when, and how to refer parents to a colleague for treatment that is outside the scope of the parent work. The timing of a successful referral is of crucial importance. It may take a parent a long period of consultation with the therapist before he or she is willing to accept a referral. The therapist also has to decide whether, in some cases, he or she can work with the parental difficulties without it hampering the child or adolescent's treatment. Some parents will not accept a referral, but they will try to gain what they can from working with the child or adolescent's therapist for personal help. Both solutions raise issues of confidentiality—if the parent is referred to a colleague should the therapist of the parent and the therapist of the child confer with each other? The issue to consider is one of confidentiality and disclosure and the effect such consultation might have on the therapists and the child or adolescent involved. In some instances, it is best for the therapist colleagues not to confer. At other times, it may be helpful for the two therapists to confer. Ethical practice requires that the therapist obtain a release from the parents and from the child, if appropriate, granting permission for the therapists to consult together. It is important to have an agreement with the parents and the patient, as appropriate, including permission and a release when the therapist of the child or adolescent plans to speak with persons about the child or adolescent beyond the parents. A further consideration is whether the parents and child or adolescent should always know when such consultations take place and the essence of what was discussed.

In ethical clinical practice, we sometimes let a dynamically driven boundary crossing exist until the parent and child are ready to address it. In one case, a mother who was narcissistically very vulnerable, with serious issues of separation from her latency-age daughter who was in intensive treatment, requested that at each appointment her daughter bring a pillow from the treatment room to the waiting room for her. In this situation, the therapist decided to permit, and to observe, this activity until the mother-daughter pair were ready to address this interaction. It was clear from the child's material that she sensed the narcissistic vulnerability of her mother. The therapist also was concerned about the mother's vulnerability and attachment to her daughter and felt that prematurely exploring the mother's behavior would lead to interruption of the treatment. This therapist's choices were to analyze with the child, to attempt to work with the mother's narcissism and separation issues, or to let this action unfold, and gradually help the daughter understand its meaning to her and to her mother. As this child worked through her own conflicts and developed her autonomy, she decided, as a result of working in treatment, to tell her mother that she did not want to bring her a pillow anymore. In this case, the mother was able to accept her daughter's decision in the context of recognizing her daughter was "getting better" and her own needs had been respected by the therapist.

Ethical issues arise in the clinical decisions we make when we, as therapists, work with the "intrusive" parent who wants to discuss her concerns in the waiting room, in the presence of the child, in the child's time, or even come into the room with the child and or adolescent or makes constant telephone calls to "fill us in." Parents who cross boundaries in this manner may be exhibiting anxieties, narcissistic vulnerabilities, insecurity, and feelings of being shut out expressed through this boundary issue. Their conflicts may result in an overprotective stance, in which they appear extraordinarily eager to provide everything possible to the therapist to help make the "therapy work." If we can understand the feelings and motivations behind these "intrusions" we can, in most cases, help these mothers and fathers feel more comfortable about not "intruding" into their children's space. We must remember, at times, these parents are demonstrating to us the wish for "overprotective" care they longed for during their own very early years. Many times parents can be helped to step back if the therapist, rather than setting limits, can understand the feelings leading to these behaviors and can help the parents find alternative ways to communicate with the therapist.

As we have seen, the therapist is engaged in relationships with multiple figures in the child or adolescent's life, most especially with the parents, on an ongoing basis. Working with confidentiality issues, the privacy of the parents and of the child and, most especially, family secrets is one of the most challenging ethical issues for the therapist. Ascherman and Rubin make this salient point,

> For the child or adolescent to use the therapeutic space freely and optimally, and for the parents or guardians to maintain sufficient trust in the analyst and process, it is crucial to clarify the distinction between privacy and secrecy at the beginning of the treatment relationship and at subsequent junctions when there is evidence that such misunderstandings of this distinction reemerge. (p. 13)

Ascherman and Rubin emphasize that on-going attention to this distinction throughout the course of the parent work is necessary. This complex work involves the therapist's deep understanding of what confidentiality means and how to work within its frame. We have touched on how the therapist can help the parents understand their child or adolescent's struggles in a general descriptive way while preserving the confidentiality of the content of what the child says and does in his or her sessions. How do we convey the parent material to the child? This is a difficult decision for the therapist. Some therapists feel it is important to tell the child everything the parents tell to them yet this can be disruptive to the process of the therapy as it may take the place of what is paramount on the child's mind. Others feel it is important to wait for relevant material in the session to emerge to gauge what is helpful to tell the child and how to tell him or her. The therapist takes into consideration the child's readiness to hear and his or her developmental level in deciding how to tell the child or adolescent what has been discussed in the parent sessions. This is often guided by the child's questions in the course of the treatment hours. If the child never asks about the parent meetings, this can be worked with as an omission on the part of the child; the therapist might wonder with the child or adolescent what makes him or her reluctant to ask.

It is helpful to anticipate the parent meeting with the child or adolescent and, at times, discuss with the child or adolescent if he/she wishes the therapist to bring up a concern or issue in the parent meetings. Conversely, it may be most helpful to work with the child toward his or her bringing his or her concerns to their parents by understanding the roots of the child or adolescent's hesitance to talk with his or her parents directly.

One way to think about issues of privacy is to understand the conflicts, defenses, and styles in a particular family and with a particular child. What do these family members feel comfortable telling one another and what do they keep private? What is appropriate for the individuals in a family to keep private? How do they speak about personal material? Is there information from the early history gleaned from parent interviews that the child needs to know to facilitate an effective treatment to proceed? Bringing such information into the treatment would be based on the developmental level of the child and his or her readiness to receive and begin to understand what is told to him or her. Examples are when to tell a child about adoption, his or her conception through in vitro fertilization, a series of miscarriages prior to the child's birth, the retardation of a sibling, a previous marriage of one of the parents, or other family matters that may be difficult for the young child to grasp. Parents can be helped by the therapist to find their own comfort with and practical ways to convey important family information to their child or adolescent. It is helpful to think of private content as part of a process which changes as the child or adolescent matures, and as the treatment deepens, so that meaningful receptivity and understanding can take place. The developmental stage of the child as well as the state of the parent-child relationship and the child or adolescent's transferences and defenses are important to consider when deciding what and when the parents and or therapist might appropriately talk with children and adolescents about sensitive material.

Family secrets present difficult ethical issues. In the treatment of children and adolescents, confronting family secrets is not uncommon. Family secrets burden the therapy of the child and place the therapist in a compromised role. At times we help parents to feel "ready" to reveal family secrets to the child whose interest would be served by his or her capacity to receive honest answers from his or her parents. We can explore the reluctance of the parents to share sensitive material with their child. Parents will sometimes tell the therapist a "family secret" and ask the therapist not to tell the child because they do not want the child to know. Some therapists will tell the parents not to reveal to them anything that they do not want their child or adolescent to know. If this is successful, it relieves the therapist of a burden and prevents the complications that occur if the therapist knows something that he or she has been requested not to tell the child or adolescent. However, this is not always the most helpful stance to take. The parents' pressure to tell the therapist a family secret may need to be respected as well. In some cases the unspoken secret may alter the course of the child or adolescent's therapy by distorting the course of the work with the parents and with their child or adolescent by limiting the therapist's understanding of the clinical material. One child who communicated only through drawing with no spoken words was trying to tell her therapist about something that appeared catastrophic in her pictorial representations. Her affects were intense, but their source was not available. The therapist felt at a loss to understand and she made several "wrong" interventions in an effort to be helpful. Several weeks later the child's parents revealed they had been contemplating divorce for some time, thinking it was best to withhold this information from their child. This "secret," now unveiled, helped this therapist communicate with her patient more helpfully. This child was disturbed by what she "knew," but was not discussed within the family. The therapist had no context in which to understand what the child wanted to communicate in her drawings, partly because communication with words was blocked by the child's conflicts over aggression, which prevented her from speaking.

One illustration of this complex problem is a case of an early adolescent whose younger sibling was dying. The parents were "good" parents, steadfast in supporting the treatment of their young daughter in the face of coping with this very painful impending loss. The parents' coping mechanisms and defenses led them to ask the therapist not to tell her patient her sibling was dying. The therapist worked with these parents to try to help them feel comfortable with her being free to talk with this early adolescent about this "secret" and to help them tell their daughter but the parents could not bring themselves to give permission for the therapist to share with her patient that she knew that her sibling was dying. The therapist felt she could not act against the parental wishes and her efforts to get permission to do so failed. This was a difficult burden for the therapist and she also was concerned her patient would lose trust in her. In this instance, when the patient's sibling died, the therapist was able to discuss with this young adolescent that she had known from the parents that her sibling was dying. The therapist worked with the meaning to her patient of her not sharing this. This young adolescent was able to work with the meaning to her of preconsciously knowing that her sibling was dying, and simultaneously knowing, preconsciously as well, that the therapist was also aware of this fact. While the patient expressed distressed feelings, the failure of the therapist's disclosure did not destroy the treatment. Some of the reasons for this were that this young adolescent grew to trust the therapist; she had worked through many of her conflicts and she had the capacity to understand her parents' ways of coping. Most importantly, however, that was the therapist and she were able to talk about the meaning of this "lapse" in disclosure to both herself and to the therapist. Should the therapist have done something differently? Was the therapist over-identified with these parents, especially the mother, because the therapist was also a mother? These questions posed difficult questions to sort out for which this therapist sought her supervisor's help in thinking through the various ramifications of her decision.

Another case presents a similar problem, from an ethical perspective, of "family secrets" from the point of view of the child or adolescent patient. This is the instance when the child or adolescent is aware of a family secret of which one parent is not. In this instance, an early adolescent girl became aware her mother was having an affair with a neighbor. She discovered this while her father was away on business when she came home early from school. This young adolescent was convinced her mother did not hear or see her (probably accurately). She went to the basement, quite upset and struggled with her curiosity and not wanting to know. Although her parents had not been getting along for some time, this daughter was still surprised. In her treatment sessions she discussed her feelings quite openly, especially her anger, but she felt in great conflict because she was attached to both parents, especially to her father. The patient feared if she said something about this to her father there would be a divorce. She feared if she told her mother, her mother would deny the event and punish her.

Yet the burden of keeping this to herself added to her already considerable stress and began to interfere with her school work. She started to show signs of regression from her hard-earned progress in her therapy. She did not hesitate to discuss this in her therapy because she trusted in the confidentiality of her therapist, but she repeatedly asked her therapist what she should do. What should the therapist do? Should he work with this adolescent's feelings about this situation and her conflicts about telling what she knows as well as her sense of betrayal, anger, guilt, and her potential oedipal conflicts aroused in this situation? Most certainly, yes. Should the therapist try to help her tell her parents what she knows? Surely not until the girl is ready. Should the therapist hold a family meeting to help this girl say what she wants to say? Not until the girl is ready and wants to participate in such a meeting. These complicated approaches require careful and thoughtful consideration by the therapist and adolescent together as the process of therapy unfolds.

An ethical response is important when the parents of a child in treatment will ask the child's therapist to treat a sibling simultaneously or after the treatment of the initial patient has ended. Alternatively, a parent may request treatment for him or herself as soon as the child's treatment has ended. Usually it seems best to preserve the "therapeutic space" in case the initial patient wishes to return to treatment in the future and to suggest that the parents find a new therapist for their second child or for themselves. This is especially true if the therapy has been a long and intensive one. The initial patient may well have feelings about his or her place being taken by a sibling or parent and may have difficulty retaining the gains of treatment or returning to the therapist. That said, with some kinds of problems such as the impact of a specific event such as a death of a sibling or parent and when the children are reacting to an external difficulty, seeing more than one child by the therapist may be very effective. Of course, in some areas, where there are few child and adolescent therapists available, it may be necessary to see more than one member of the family. In this case, the therapist needs to pay particular attention to issues of confidentiality, privacy, and secrets. Again, paying careful attention to the meaning and effects of "doubling" in therapy is central to making this arrangement work.

Outside the office contacts require ethically grounded decisions by the therapist. A child or adolescent and/or a parent will sometimes ask the therapist to come to his or her birthday party, games, play, graduation, or other family event. The ethical principle involved is consideration of the effect on the child or adolescent patient to decline or to accept the invitation. This decision depends upon the theoretical perspective of the therapist and his or her understanding of the dynamic meaning of the invitation to the child or adolescent. Usually, it may be best to help the child or adolescent understand the therapeutic reasons for declining to come and the meaning to the child of the therapist's not accepting the invitation. Parent education around these issues is also important. Certainly the child or adolescent's disappointment, puzzlement, and feelings of rejection need to be thoughtfully worked with. Some therapists feel attending these events is in the service of supporting the child or adolescent's development. In some cases, this could be true, and in others, it is a rationalization by the therapist who wants to be included in the patient's family for conscious or unconscious reasons. Therapists who are less aware of their own feelings are more likely to slip into becoming "part of the family," which is not helpful to and may interfere with the treatment. Chance encounters outside the therapeutic situation with parents requires courteous behavior on the part of the therapist with appreciation of the various meanings these encounters may have for these parents.

An ethical professional stance is particularly necessary when the therapist is confronted with personal stressful issues, which may threaten his or her professional life. Illnesses and significant stresses in the life of the therapist that affect or disrupt the treatment, require careful and thoughtful attention by the therapist as to the effect of his or her situation on his or her child and adolescent patients as well as upon their parents. The meaning of what is happening to the therapist will vary among patients depending on their age, developmental and family history, and the psychological issues alive in the treatment. Consultation with a colleague can provide important perspectives for an ill or stressed therapist to think through ways of working with each patient and his or her parents to minimize the impact of his or her life circumstance on the children, adolescents, and their families. The therapist must work with the parents to make the best treatment arrangements for their child and to assist them in handling this unexpected situation with their child or adolescent. The consultation will also prove helpful to the therapist who needs help in thinking through the best way to take care of him or herself while doing their best for the parents and patients. In some instances, therapists with a terminal illness continue to practice beyond the point of effectiveness which may be detrimental to the patient. Consultation with a colleague is especially helpful in making the painful decision to close a practice before this point is reached.

Therapists are at the beginning stages of confronting the new issues in professional practice raised by the entry of technology into the treatment process and space. In this technological age, therapists are confronted with the pros and cons of communicating with parents by e-mail. Many parents will communicate more fully with the therapist by e-mail than by phone or in-person visits. Sometimes they will communicate too much or use the e-mail to air their own problems. E-mail communication may serve as an effective defense against discussing problems in parenting that the parents do not want to face in person with their child's therapist. The e-mail provides a distance that may protect the parents from their own feelings and demonstrate reticence in forming a relationship with the therapist.

Communication with parents by e-mail can result in breaches of confidentiality and privacy on the part of the therapist and the parents. The confidentiality of the therapist-patient relationship is of prime concern when communicating by e-mail. Pressing the wrong command by mistake could expose a patient and his or her family to an e-mail audience, which could cause irreparable harm.

The therapist may also use e-mail as a defense against their reluctance to meet with the parents, especially those who are difficult and who touch on conflicts and vulnerabilities in the therapist. Often, it is easier for both the parents and the therapist not to meet in person. The therapist needs to carefully consider the dynamic meanings, the effect of e-mail communication, the potential breaches of confidentiality, and privacy as well as the impact on the essential purpose of the work with the parents before deciding what stance to take regarding this form of communication.

The numerous invasions to our patients' and their families' privacy raise ethical questions and concerns for therapists of children and adolescents. Therapists of children and adolescents are frequently asked for information about their patients from schools, camps, and third-party payers. These requests are often necessary to enable the child to participate in school and camp activities or for parents to receive reimbursement from insurance companies. Many parents are hesitant to have the therapist supply any information about their children as they do not want the child to have a record of psychological treatment. The therapist discusses these concerns with the parents and works with them to fulfill the required information in a way that does not prejudice the child or adolescent. As with conveying what the child is struggling with to the parents, the therapist and parents together can work to provide information that will fulfill the purpose of the request, by stating the information in the most minimal and general terms. The child and adolescent should be fully informed and involved in this process as appropriate to his or her developmental stage. The therapist should always have the informed consent of the parents and of the child or adolescent before submitting any information to a school, camp, or insurance company. Most often, if the therapist works closely with the parents and the patient, eliciting from them what information they would feel comfortable about submitting, the requirements can be fulfilled without breaching confidentiality in a way harmful to the family or the child and adolescent.

Ethical questions may arise over the issue of medication for children and adolescents. Parents may request or demand that the therapist medicate their child, especially if the child or adolescent's behavior is overtly disturbing to the parents or to the school. When the need for such intervention is inconclusive or inadvisable, the therapist can work with the parents to help them postpone this decision for further assessment. The therapist will also explain the pros and cons and effects of medication on the child and on the therapeutic work. The therapist needs to understand the reasons for the parents' request which sometimes comes from misconceptions about medication or from deeper reasons within the parents themselves. Often it is useful to suggest a second opinion to the parents which can be very helpful in making decisions about medication. Consultation with a professional trained and experienced in the psychopharmacological treatment of children and adolescents is often helpful. While we can understand the parents or teachers desire for immediate relief of symptoms through medication, deciding to medicate a child or adolescent must be based on a comprehensive evaluation of all the factors involved.

How does the therapist work with parents who request a particular diagnosis in order to obtain services from a school that might benefit the child but is an incorrect diagnosis? Parents are eager for their child or adolescent to do well in school and they frequently press for testing and diagnoses that might, for example, give their students extra time on tests. If such a diagnosis or testing is not clinically indicated the therapist could work with the parents of these children to help them understand that their anxieties about their child are displaced onto school performance rather than being understood, perhaps, as issues of parental narcissism and competitiveness with other parents.

The therapist faces a very difficult situation when parents consult them about a child who has been or is suspected to have been molested by a previous nanny, babysitter, or teacher. The parents do not want to press charges but are eager to have their child in treatment. These parents often feel guilty about what happened to their child. Sometimes they are blind to the fact that they did not know or see their child was being mistreated under their eyes, which sometimes points to pathology or the repetition of a parental experience of molestation as a child. The ethical obligation of the therapist presents a conflict for him or her. Reporting the molestation, especially if it is recent or even ongoing, may lead the parents to pull their child out of treatment. The relationship of the child or adolescent to the therapist may also be compromised by this action on the part of the therapist. Yet, the therapist is legally required to report molestation to Child Protective Services. The first step to solve this dilemma is to work with the parents on their perceptions, guilt, fears, and sorrows about what happened and help them to do the required reporting. If this approach fails, the therapist must inform the parents of what is required of him or her by law and act accordingly. It is not helpful to the parents to experience the therapist as evading his or her responsibility as they themselves may be.

Ethical practice demands that the therapist be self-aware of the functioning of his or her own conscience to prevent ethical problems from arising. We need to be familiar with our vulnerabilities, tendencies to rationalize, and pulls toward self-interest such as financial concerns. We also need to be aware of the times when we need outside help to think through a difficult ethical dilemma, when we have questions about our decisions, or when we are "bothered" by a clinical situation that continues to trouble us and we cannot resolve for ourselves. Ongoing self-monitoring and interaction with colleagues around ethical issues helps reinforce our ethical stance. As ethical issues arise in daily clinical moments we address them within our ethical frame and with our professional ethical ego ideal to guide us in the moment.

REFERENCES

Ascherman, L., M.D. and Rubin, S. (2009). *Ethical and professional concerns in child and adult psychoanalysis*. Unpublished manuscript.

Study Group Discussions. Cope Study Group on Supervision in Child and Adolescent Psychoanalysis. The American Psychoanalytic Association.

FOUR

Ethical Considerations in the Supervisor-Supervisee Relationship and the Supervisory Process

Ethical principles and practice affect many aspects of the supervision of therapy and analysis with children and adolescents. The complex conscious and unconscious communications of the supervisor with the supervisee, and the supervisee's interaction with child or adolescent patient and the patient's parents open opportunities for transference reactions to intrude, disruption of the frame and ethical lapses. We will examine some of these potential areas for interferences of the therapeutic frame and ways to prevent potential difficulties.

At first glance, supervision of clinical work helps the student therapist to integrate theory and practice. It provides the student with new ways of listening, so that the child patient's multiple modes of communication can be understood. Further, supervision helps the student to formulate useful interventions, so children of all ages can benefit from the interaction between the therapist and themselves.

In clinical supervision of work with children and adolescents, the trainee learns to establish a therapeutic frame. This refers to the manner in which treatment is conducted with respect to practices of consistency, such as predictable and stable length and frequency of sessions, fees to which parents and therapist agree, level of privacy the child or adolescent patient can anticipate, and all factors that contribute to a stable structure for the treatment. It is in the area of maintaining the frame that lapses in ethical principles and practices are most frequent and prominent.

While guidelines for ethical practice with child and adolescent patients and their parents are frequently conveyed, in some form, during the course of supervision of clinical cases, standards for ethical behavior in the relationship between supervisor and supervisee receive somewhat less attention. We will address this during the course of our examination of the multidimensional process of supervision.

Ethical behavior that is sustained and reliable involves more than simply following prescribed guidelines, but thinking about the manifestations of those impulses, some unconscious, for which those prohibitions and injunctions were initially established. A supervisor of therapy can direct the student therapist's attention to behaviors that suggest the potential for ethical lapses. For example, a student therapist reports his young adolescent female patient wanted to dance with him, and given the patient's past history with abusive relationships, the student deemed this behavior a "corrective emotional experience." In this instance, the supervisor can examine the implications of such an activity in the context of therapy with the student. This exploration might include the nature of the patient's transference, the student therapist's countertransference responses, and ethical issues as well.

FOR DISCUSSION

- What are the ethical implications of the interplay between supervisor and supervisee, assuming that the transaction has both conscious and unconscious elements?
- At what cost does the supervisor protect the sensibilities of the student therapist?
- How may it affect the student's future work with child and adolescent patients?

Supervision of one's clinical work, in addition to being enormously helpful in one's work with child and adolescent patients and their parents, may leave the student feeling concerned about faculty criticism and career progression. Ideally, interaction between supervisor and student takes place in a collegial atmosphere (Kernberg). When this is the case, the function of noncompetitive mutual respect in supervision enables the student to engage fruitfully in reporting what took place between him/her and the child patient or the patient's parents. In this context, the student feels free enough to report interventions of which he/she feels doubt, dissatisfaction, or anticipates that the supervisor might assess as suboptimal.

The supervisor, in many training situations, sends reports on the supervisee's work to the institute. Currently, most students have access to these reports and may discuss them with her/his supervisor. At times, the degree to which students have access to reports affects what the supervisor is willing to write about the student's clinical abilities. If the student is too intimidated because of personal conflicts or institute politics to offer accurate accounts of what took place in the child's treatment, or in consultation with the parent, his or her education suffers. Ultimately, the patient may not receive optimal care.

Further, the student who fears losing a case may attempt to conceal some of what transpires between her or him and the patient. He or she may behave, consciously or unconsciously, in a subtly seductive manner with the child and/or the parents, he or she may fail to deal with the patient's aggression, or may agree to a fee that is unrealistically low. This is another example in which the process of supervision is compromised, as is the care of the child or patient. Alternatively, the student may be overly aggressive, restraining a child patient more than necessary if she/he feels threatened by the child's behavior. It is important that considerable attention be directed toward the therapy student's experience of a safe environment for discussing clinical practice. It is helpful when both supervisor and supervisee recognize the ethical implications of these "supervisory problems" of honesty and integrity.

It is also crucial for supervisor and student therapist to recognize ethical issues in supervision that are encumbered by transferences of both parties. The therapy student's transference responses to the supervisor are complex and multidetermined. When the student fails to reflect upon and examine his/her transference responses to the supervisor, he or she may respond to the supervisor's comments in a wide variety of ways, consciously inexplicable. Given this situation, the effects of the supervisor's suggestions might be accepted or rejected in a facile manner and the patient's treatment is not likely to be optimal.

While a full examination of the trainee's transferences in the supervisory situation are best addressed in the student's personal treatment, an alert supervisor may help the student to initially identify such internal struggles. For example, in the supervision of a child or adolescent patient, the therapy student might perceive the supervisor as representing an aspect of his/her personal therapist or his/her parent of early childhood. This process is typically unconscious. In contrast, the supervisory situation may be perceived by the student as reminiscent of a particularly challenging moment from his/her early life. One effect of such unconscious conflict might be that the student may respond to a benign supervisory comment with intense and conflicted feelings that are not appropriate to the situation.

A similar situation may take place with the supervisor and his/her transferences to the student. A supervisor may anticipate that a student, toward whom he/she has unconscious transference feelings, perhaps who reminds him of someone from his past, will accommodate him to an unrealistic degree. The supervisor may wish to serve as "an exception" in the student's life, with no attention to ethical principles. The wide variety of reported cases of ethical lapses in the supervisory situation must lead one to be vigilant and forthright, and to seek consultation if the circumstances appear to require this.

In view of all of our concerns about potential difficulties in supervision, do we imply that the risk of working with a student or trainee is too great? This is certainly not the case. We are simply identifying particular vulnerabilities so students and candidates may address them in supervision, thoughtfully and critically. As a result of this crucial work, the student therapist for children and adolescents may substantively improve the quality of his/her clinical work.

Given the multitude of transference issues that may arise during supervision, we find that the therapist who has engaged productively in his/her own treatment is generally in a better position to encounter the challenges of working with children and adolescents. While students of psychoanalysis are required to engage in personal analysis during the course of their training, many child therapists in training also elect to do so when they recognize the value of this endeavor as part of their education in learning to treat children and adolescents. An understanding of one's own conflicts and defenses is invaluable in the therapist's efforts to understand otherwise "inexplicable" responses of the child patient or their parents. Such understanding is useful in the supervisory interaction as well, and may help the student to use such educational opportunities more productively. Treating children and adolescents, when one has no experience in exploring personal conflicts in therapy, increases the risk of ethical lapses and violations.

What is the ethical principle in the following example?

When a supervisor suggests a particular intervention or interpretation for the student therapist to offer to a child or an adolescent patient, he or she should discuss with the supervisee what are his/her feelings about making the suggested intervention, at least in their early work together. The astute supervisor is alert to the student who dutifully makes a suggested interpretation while remaining unconvinced of the validity of the comment. In this case, the personal conflicts of the student prevent him/her from using education in supervision, the child receives inadequate treatment, and the ethical issue is clear.

For some therapy students, the suggestion of making a particular interpretation to the child patient may be experienced as "too aggressive." Again, it is incumbent upon the student to question what feels uncomfortable and continue to examine this material until he or she fully grasps the value of the proposed intervention.

With respect to ethical practice, the student therapist is preparing for a career of working with relative independence. He/she must have the maturity, integrity, and self-reflective capacities to respect what he/she observes both in the clinical situation with the child patient and that which takes place in supervisory sessions. The student who dutifully follows direction in an unquestioning manner is not behaving in an ethically-principled manner. If these issues are addressed directly early in training, they are less likely to become problematic.

In our experience, the nature of the wide variety of transferences between student and supervisor is frequently not given the attention it deserves. Since this has great impact upon the supervisee's training and consequently upon the child patient's treatment, we recommend that it become a far greater part of work in both supervision and coursework that addresses therapeutic work with child and adolescent patients and their parents.

Ethical challenges to the student therapist presented by families include demands for a particular diagnosis to satisfy an insurance company, for a particular medication, perhaps to please a teacher who has diagnosed ADHD, or to offer frequency of treatment that is not optimal but is suggested as a way of "keeping the case."

In this case, the supervisor may take up the challenge and work with both the practical reality and the ethical questions. Alternatively, the supervisor may simply offer a way of behaving that "satisfies everyone" and fail to attend to the ethical dilemmas that the student therapist confronts. Since few courses on ethics in treating children and adolescents are offered in programs of child therapy and child analysis (see appendix for an outline for a suggested course), work in supervision can help the candidate or trainee to examine this material from a wide variety of vantage points.

With respect to the supervisor/supervisee situation, are mutual vulnerabilities really reciprocal?

We referred earlier to the supervisee's idealization of the supervisor, a process that has substantive unconscious components. This may lead the supervisee to seek more than the supervisor can provide. Similarly, when the supervisor idealizes the student, he/she may expect more than the student can offer, in terms of clinical skill and a multitude of other factors. When the unconscious components are prominent, this opens the way for unexplained anger, disappointment, and unethical behavior. For example, a student therapist may invite the supervisor to treat his/her family member. If the supervisor agrees to this, there are potential ethical difficulties in terms of potential for boundary violation. Under what circumstances might this be viable? In some cases, if the student is no longer in supervision, and there is no further communication about the patient without the patient's permission, it can be.

Still, the situation is fraught with difficulty and it is preferable for the supervisee to find another trusted therapist, with whom he/she is not in close contact, to treat the family member. If the supervisor and super visee live in a small town where no other viable therapy is possible, the circumstances are somewhat altered.

What of the reverse? When the supervisor idealizes the supervisee and invites his/her student to treat a family member, this situation is much more likely to result in boundary issues for a multitude of reasons.

It is the ethical responsibility of the supervisor to maintain the frame of supervision as a professional relationship in which the student is particularly vulnerable because of transferences. When the supervisor, in a position of psychological and political power, takes advantage of the power differential and the student's transferences and asks of the student that which is too demanding, unrealistic, or unethical, the burden of behaving in a principled manner belongs, in greater proportion, to the supervisor, upon whom the student depends for guidance. This does not exempt the student from thoughtful examination of that which is asked of him/her but simply addresses the risks that take place in a situation of unequal power and manifestations of transference.

With respect to the supervisor/supervisee relationship, transferences and countertransferences lead to other forms of ethical lapses as well. Each may experience positive transference to the other and ultimately share personal information that is far beyond that which is relevant to the case being presented.

Examples of unethical behavior include the supervisor's speaking with the supervisee about his/her patients, initially from a clinical perspective and later in merely conveying gossip. Acting on unresolved, and unexamined, transference conflicts opens the way to indiscretions. When the regression is prominent in the student therapist, his/her wish to please the supervisor may take precedence over principled behavior.

Alternatively, when supervisor and supervisee share particular "blind spots," they may both "hate the parents" of a child or adolescent patient and fail to have a balanced perspective of people who are struggling with their children who are in conflict.

ETHICAL ISSUES

While the supervisor is able to point out unconscious impulses, and defenses against such impulses to the student who has had an experience of exploratory therapy, he or she may be less able to do so with the therapist who has declined to engage in personal therapy. The ethical problem is that, when transactions between patient and therapist are viewed as exclusively "on the surface," there may be greater propensity for acting-out of unconscious or preconscious impulses than when the therapist is aware of what motivates him/her. The therapy student must identify and work at his/her tendencies to overestimate his teacher/supervisor. When the supervisor simply enjoys the student's overvaluation and fails to examine what role it might have in the student's treatment of patients, treatment is suboptimal.

Part of the task of the supervisor in child and adolescent analysis, is to help the student to think about ethical dilemmas. When the trainee presents specific problems, it may appear simpler to merely offer a mode of behavior, but it is of far greater value to identify the ethical issue and explore it in great detail, allowing the student to struggle with matters of conscience. For example, the parents ask, "Our insurance company won't pay for 'parent consultations' even though they are an essential part of the treatment, so will you falsify your bill and indicate that parent consultations were actually treatment sessions for our child?"

In another example, a parent may ask the student therapist to assign a diagnosis that is incorrect so that particular services from the school will become available. Or a student therapist may be asked to medicate a child "to make the parents happy," even if this is not clinically indicated.

The role of the supervisor in discussing these issues is pivotal in the student's development. Does the supervisor make every effort to understand the student's dilemma: to keep parents from getting angry, to "keep the case" and prevent premature termination, to avoid aggression? Examining the material in detail is more useful than simply offering a directive, i.e., "Do this." "Don't do this."

When the student has a solid basis for understanding the ethical principles involved, he or she develops the foundations for a career that is ethically based and principled. To the degree to which the student understands impulses for ethical lapses, and impulses in therapists that lead to articulated codes of ethical behavior, the student's standards for ethical behavior will be based on a solid foundation and will serve him/her in an enduring manner.

A question that frequently arises in matters of ethical dilemmas is, "Who has ultimate responsibility for the patient?" Is it the treating therapist, the supervisor, or the training institute? Is the responsibility shared? Kernberg points out the importance of making this clear and explicit. This dilemma is underscored when the case involves, for example, a child or adolescent patient whose risky behavior may lead to disastrous results. In such cases, another matter of ethical concern is, "What material is shared with parents and what aspects of it remain in the consultation/supervision?" How does the therapist or analyst work with this when the child or adolescent patient resists contact between parent and therapist or analyst?

In an analysis, one may examine with the adolescent, for example, the nature of her/his provocative and risky behavior, the feelings he/she wishes to stir in those who know of the behavior, such as the analyst, and the feelings the patient wishes to arouse in those who do not know, such as the parents? The therapist may also examine in himself or herself whether the child or adolescent's behavior is enjoyed, unconsciously and vicariously, by the treating individual. Is the therapist perceived as agreeing with the adolescent's provocative behavior by keeping it secret?

When all of this is examined, and resistance to sharing the problem with parents is still present, the therapist's ethical principles may dictate that this sharing of information is a precondition for continuing treatment. This raises an ethical question to be examined from multiple perspectives, in study groups and seminars.

When the adolescent's behavior does not involve a threat to safety, the examination of the feelings, in depth, may result in more autonomy for the adolescent patient, a greater reliance on her/his conscience, and deeper development of a personal sense of ethics.

With respect to distinctions between psychotherapy and psychoanalysis, if behavior changes as a result of a process of understanding and progressive development, it can be more enduring than if the essential tool is the idealizing transference, i.e., the changes are due to respect and admiration from the therapist and the adolescent is "persuaded" to behave differently.

There are many instances when, in dynamic psychotherapy, a skilled child therapist can help the child or adolescent make changes that result from an understanding of transference and resistances, and the change is enduring. It is important to recognize when, in particular cases, the treatment of choice is psychotherapy.

Overall, supervision has the potential to be a crucial, positive, and mutual learning experience with enduring results. If the student is left with a lifelong interest in asking crucial questions, in wondering what forms of interactions are most beneficial to the child or adolescent patient and his/her parents, then supervision has, at least in part, fulfilled its promise.

To continue our examination of ethical dilemmas, at times the student therapist of children—when not engaged in personal therapy—may bring up his/her own personal conflicts during the course of supervisory work for the child patient. When there is a blurring of boundaries, so that supervisor and supervisee are both engaged in the patient's productions, and simultaneously engaged in friendship and/or a personal therapeutic relationship, the result is a failure to attend to unconscious phenomena that may adversely affect work with the patient. The ethical problem is that unconscious phenomena taking place between student therapist and supervisor may deprive the patient of optimal care. This takes place when boundaries are blurred between supervision, treatment, and personal relationship.

In addition to the unconscious conflicts, there are real pressures upon students to conform to institutional theories. The candidate in child analysis may fear authority and fear deviating from the accepted technical approaches at her/his institute. Just as the student may fear discussing an alternative approach, the supervisor may have concern that his/her colleagues will be critical of the supervision of a candidate/student who does not do well. Multiple factors are at work here.

Intense disappointment of the student with the supervisor places in jeopardy the treatment of the child or adolescent patient. The ethical problem of jeopardizing a patient's therapy because the student therapist failed to seek his/her own treatment is substantial. While the supervisor may want to help a student in distress, it is best to refer the student for treatment if there are ongoing difficulties that distract attention from the matter at hand: the treatment of the child.

When the supervisee displays pathology that is a clear interference with his/her ability to function as a therapist, it is the ethical responsibility of the supervisor to bring this to the student's attention. If further action is required, the supervisor may ask that the student refrain from treating patients until the student's issues are resolved in a satisfactory manner. In such cases, which are not common, this may involve the supervisor helping the student to transfer patients to another therapist, so that they will not be subjected to the pathology of the student.

What is the ethical responsibility of both supervisor and institute when the student therapist's skill is insufficient to work with a particular child or adolescent patient?

In some cases, it is necessary, from an ethical perspective, for the supervisor to help the student to transfer the care of the patient to another therapist. This necessarily involves narcissistic injury of the therapist, but for the health of the patient it is the most judicious and ethical pathway.

It is well known among experienced supervisors that a parallel process frequently takes place, in which the nature of the interaction between supervisor and student reflects, albeit in an unconscious manner, that which is occurring between student and child or adolescent patient or between student and the parent of the child or adolescent who is being treated.

For example, if the child patient is wildly throwing about toys and the student-therapist feels endangered, the student, during supervision, may unconsciously create a situation in which the supervisor feels threatened. This takes place in a psychological mode, not a physical one.

If the parents of the child who is being treated take the position that the student must "do something at once" to help their child, the student therapist may come to supervision, or even to a case conference, and unconsciously create a situation in which an individual who hears the case material experiences the same urgency. Of course, in some cases the urgency is actually present, but frequently it is an unconscious pressure that is experienced by the treating person and conveyed to those who are trying to offer help with the technique in the case.

ETHICAL DILEMMAS IN THE SUPERVISORY SITUATION

Dr. "C" continuously "dozed" in supervision, while his supervisees spoke of this with each other but feared speaking with Dr. "C" directly. One student indicated that he had "solved the problem" by bringing Dr. "C" coffee at each supervision. Soon, the supervisor became sleepy again and the student would "bring donuts." Finally a conscientious student confronted the supervisor, who was forced to face his difficulties directly.

Dr. "Y" was seductive with female supervisees, asking to date them and complaining that his wife "didn't understand." Once again, a series of supervisees felt obliged to comply, until one reported this to another supervisor, who helped her to address the problem both with the supervisor and the institute.

The feelings of helplessness of the supervisee have a ripple effect, and adversely affect work with patients, who then suffer at the hands of a therapist who feels victimized. One particular challenge of supervision is to recognize, and attend to, various layers of unconscious defenses. These include the defenses of the student therapist, the child or adolescent patient, the patient's parents, and the supervisor her/himself. This is arduous work.

Unconscious defenses are essentially "blind spots," and failure to recognize and work with them may lead to ethical lapses. For this reason, constant self-scrutiny on the part of the supervisor is required so that the supervisory experience is successful, while maintaining an open environment for communication. In this context, consultation and group supervision are also helpful in identifying areas of unawareness in the supervisory relationship.

What is the ethical principle in this case?

A psychology intern, in her own treatment, and in a phase of strongly positive transference, begins supervision. She feels that she loves her supervisor, would even prefer the supervisor as therapist, and she accepts all recommendations uncritically. The supervisor, in this case of a nine-year-old boy, misunderstands some of the student's communications and recommends that she offer a particular intervention to the boy. She feels "this doesn't sound right, but my supervisor recommended it." She makes the intervention and the boy becomes profoundly depressed. After weeks, there is clarification of the situation and the boy's depression lifts. With respect to ethics, in this case a patient suffered unduly because his student therapist accepted uncritically the suggestion of a venerated figure.

From an ethical perspective, the potential difficulties are patent.

When there is open communication, and the supervisor is aware of the student's idealization, he or she may raise questions, such as, "Does this suggestion seem appropriate to the clinical material?" "What intervention would you make?" "Perhaps we can examine some of the ways in which your patient might interpret this intervention."

On the part of the student, this requires constant self-scrutiny, i.e., "Am I following this advice because it appears most consistent with the material?" "Does the suggested intervention appear out of context and am I simply 'obeying' because of my wish to comply with an idealized teacher?" "Am I hoping for referrals from this supervisor and therefore hesitating to question his/her suggestions?" These questions are only the beginning of one's learning to work safely and in the best interest of the patient and her/his parent.

What is the ethical principle here?

Ethics in working with children and their parents include maintaining a professional relationship of teaching and learning. The complication of this situation with the treatment of the relative of someone who is perceived more from a perspective of transference than in reality, can only come to an unfortunate end.

Case example of an ethical dilemma

When the supervisor has a response, perhaps unconsciously, to the child and/or the parents who are being treated by his supervisee, this may provide an impediment to supervision and may lead to ethical problems. For example, a therapy student complained that parents of a five year old appear uncooperative, arrive late, and sometimes fail to call for their child in a timely manner. The student neglected to inform the supervisor that the young patient's father was dying and that the mother was preoccupied with visits to her father some distance from home.

The supervisor responded angrily toward the mother, unconsciously motivated by anger with his own early experience with his mother, and did not question the student's presentation and offered suggestions for the student's approach to the parents that were aggressive, punitive, and entirely inappropriate. The result was that the child's treatment was interrupted, although he made enormous progress with respect to development and conflict resolution, and was engaged in a sustained positive transference. This patient found it impossible to trust future therapists for many years following this traumatic interruption.

Supervision of child and adolescent therapy and analysis is arduous work, and the supervisor must be aware of his/her impulses to react impulsively to material presented. When the supervisor reacts unconsciously, without careful examination of material, we find that this leads to ethical lapses. Treatments of children and adolescents are interrupted and patients suffer unnecessarily.

ETHICAL CONSIDERATIONS OF SUPERVISION OF THE PRIVACY IN THERAPY

Treatment begins with the therapist respecting the fact that the child has her/his "own mind" and that thoughts, feelings, and fantasies expressed in treatment are to remain private. This permits the child or adolescent patient to establish trust, which is crucial in psychological development and in progress of treatment.

When the therapist shares information about a child or adolescent's treatment with parents and keeps this fact "secret" from the patient, the motives may be multidetermined. For example, a student therapist may experience "pressure" about the parent's wish to be "included" in the treatment. The student may want to conceal feelings of incompetence and use revealing of private material as diversion. Alternatively, the student may want to pacify the parent who is irritated about the course of treatment, or the student may experience the parent as his/her own parent of early childhood and wish to be both "obedient/disobedient."

It is the role of the supervisor to work with the student about what is being conveyed to the parents and why this is being done. How does the student understand his communications to parents? How might the parents interpret the communication by the treating therapist? How does the student therapist experience this in relation to the supervisor? How does he/she understand it in relation to the student's own relation with her/his parents in childhood? Is the supervisee developing his own method, or is he/she feeling too pressed to work in the manner of the supervisor without fully understanding the principles involved? Is the supervisor conveying a need to keep trust while, in personal life, behaving as a gossip? What is the nature of identification in the communications between supervisor and supervisee, supervisee and child and parent? A clear ability to address this provides a beginning for an environment in which therapeutic action can take place.

Note

These questions are intended to stimulate fruitful discussions that can take place both during one's training and later. Naturally the level of experience of the therapist will affect the depth to which one considers these matters, not insignificantly.

Breaking the trust of a child or adolescent by revealing private information to parents is an impediment to treatment in both the current situation and in future treatments. When matters are revealed to parents, such as details of fantasies that the child expressed in treatment, and this is repeated by the parent in a moment of anger, the child's trust is disrupted and their development may be affected.

What of the adolescent who is engaging in risky behavior? To what degree does maintaining privacy have priority?

The supervisee must understand and convey to the adolescent patient that, while communication in therapy is for the most part confidential, under particular circumstances of danger parents must be called into the conversation. The supervisee's hesitancy must be understood in this context:

- Does she/he fear the parents? Fear the supervisor?
- Does the student therapist fear losing his/her patient's trust and destroying the treatment? Is he/she repeating an experience of adolescence in which risky behavior took place and parents were either unaware or overly intrusive?
- Does the child therapist compete with the child patient's parents so that he/she will be perceived by the patient as "more understanding?"
- Does the therapist want so much to please the adolescent patient that ethical responsibility for what is kept private becomes invisible?
- Does the supervisor fear having the student "lose the case" and so fail to insist that parents be included in the conversation when the patient is in danger?
- Is the supervisor overly fearful, personally, and therefore recommending that parents be called at every misdeed of a neurotic adolescent?
- Is the supervisor reliving a risk-taking time in adolescence and vicariously enjoying the patient's indulging in life-threatening behavior?
- Is the same true for the supervisee?
- Is supervisor or supervisee feeling so omnipotent, recalling their own adolescence, that they do not feel the need to invite parents into the conversation itself?

Confronting each of these issues, and how they change during the course of treatment, is central to good supervision in which ethical considerations are foremost.

When the supervisor defensively identifies with parents and he/she offers interventions for the child or adolescent that appear to be less empathic and thoughtful and more punitive, it is crucial that he/she examine the unconscious motives that are driving the suggested intervention.

FEES

Setting fees when working with child and adolescent patients is a complex matter, particularly when the fee is reduced. This is frequently the case when the therapist is a student in training. Should the child contribute some part of the cost, for example, if she/he is an adolescent and is engaged in some part time employment, such as babysitting? Opinions vary, and most important is open discussion and working to understand the meanings of this, as they arise in the course of treatment.

How does the student assess what parents are able to afford, yet is still within the boundaries of what would be a reasonable fee? What is the fee for supervision, and how do supervisor and student agree to this? Is silent resentment over supervisory fee carried into the fee that the patient's parents are charged? These factors are determined both consciously and unconsciously, with respect to what the student pays for her/his own therapy, and supervision. Additionally, unconscious elements include the student's views of monetary exchange from early childhood. If there is major discrepancy between financial circumstances of supervisor, student, patient, and parents, unconscious factors may appear in an insidious manner. Does the student envy the child or adolescent's wealth, or feel sorry for the child or adolescent who has few advantages and extend themselves in a manner that is not sustainable?

How are fees discussed early in supervision from an ethical perspective?

Are they related to the student's own ability to pay as well as that of his/her patient? What takes place when parents stop paying the bill for treatment? Do one's ethical principles continue to respect the child or adolescent's treatment and still call parents to task when they fail to meet responsibilities? Each of these matters can be discussed in substantive ways in seminars and study groups from the perspective of ethical guidelines.

If the child's treatment continues after the student graduates from a child therapy training program, how does the recently graduated child and adolescent therapist consider changes in fee? Does he/she raise the fee precipitously so that the child patient can no longer continue in treatment? This would represent unethical behavior and should be monitored by the student's self-analysis, consultation, and peer supervision. Psychotherapeutic work with children and their parents is far more complex, in many ways, than work with adults, since arrangements of beginning treatment, of time, and fee, are made with someone other than the primary patient. For this reason, the child/adolescent may suffer when there is disagreement about purpose of treatment, fees, structure of treatment, and the child is left out of the discussion. Therefore, at what point must child or adolescent be included in such discussion?

Obviously this varies with the age of the child, the level of development, his ability to grasp the circumstances, and the flexibility of the parents. To what degree is the form of treatment based upon what the family can "afford?" That is, if intensive therapy is most suitable for a particular child or adolescent, what are the ethical implications of offering less intensive treatment when the student therapist "does not want a low fee?" How does the supervisor discuss options, such as referring the child or adolescent to a clinic setting, in which optimal treatment might be available at a fee that the family can afford?

The overriding issue in maintaining ethical principles in treating children and adolescents is one of considering what is best for the patient. The therapist who engages in self-reflection and recognizes that unconscious factors influence our behavior is much more likely to offer treatment that is successful and enduring. It is in this context that good clinical technique and ethical practices are fully integrated.

REFERENCES

Jacobs, D., Paul, D., Meyer, D.J. (1995). *The supervisory encounter*. New Haven, CT: Yale University Press.

Kernberg, Otto F. (2010). "Psychoanalytic supervision: The supervisor's tasks." *Psychoanalytic Quarterly*, Volume LXXIX, No. 3. pp. 603-627.

Thomas, J. T. (2010). *The ethics of supervision and consultation: Practical guidance for mental health professionals*. Washington D.C.: American Psychological Association.

FIVE

Ethical and Forensic Aspects of Work with Children and their Families

Moisy Shopper, M.D.

This chapter deals with ethical issues in forensic work with children, adolescents, and their families. Matters of court testimony, custody decisions, and psychological evaluation of children for the legal system are addressed. For the child therapist who thinks in terms of unconscious conflicts and defenses, the notion of testifying in court about matters of custody raises substantive questions with respect to privacy, confidentiality, and trust. Alternatively, there is an ethical dilemma about an obligation to participate in the legal system when one can offer an alternative viewpoint that may be helpful in making crucial decisions that affect child welfare.

ETHICAL IMPLICATIONS OF CUSTODY DECISIONS

In 2000, three child analysts became prominent in the popular media when Elian Gonzalez, floating in a rubber tube, was picked up by fishermen and brought to Florida. His mother and her boyfriend had fled from Cuba in a five foot aluminum boat with eight other passengers. Elian and two others were the only survivors. The Cuban exiles vociferously advocated that Elian stay with his somewhat distant relatives in Florida, while the U.S. courts, after reviewing the report of Paulina Kernberg, M.D., decided in favor of his being reunited with his father in Cuba. Diane Sawyer, host on *Good Morning America,* asked analyst Gunther Perdigao to assist her in interviewing Elian (personal communication). In his assessment of Elian's state, Dr. Perdigao asked the boy to draw pictures and to talk about his drawing. Some child analysts were critical of Dr. Perdigao's assessment of the boy, since they felt that his method, while analytically informed, did not fully evaluate Elian's inner life or provide a thorough evaluation of the situation. Humberto Nagera, M.D., wrote a paper (unpublished) supporting Elian's remaining with his great uncle and his family in the U.S. (personal communication). From the perspective of the media, the legal and political arguments were far more prominent than the psychological understanding of the boy's plight.

A column by Erica Goode of the *New York Times* (2000) summarized the work of the psychological professionals who received substantial attention in the case. While all three analysts were fluent in Spanish, Dr. Kernberg, a former citizen of Chile, was selected to offer the most influential opinion because, at that time, she was the director of a well-respected program that investigated problems of divorce and its impact upon children, particularly with respect to helping children to cope with custody changes. In addition, Dr. Kernberg had substantive experience in preparing reports and expert testimony for the courts.

Partly in response to this unforeseen prominence of child analysts in the media, the American Psychoanalytic Association developed programs to assist analysts in presenting their work to the public and to the press. In general, child analysts and analytically informed child therapists do not routinely become involved in legal matters, partly out of concern for protecting confidentiality of patients. For this reason, a biased version of psychodynamic approaches finds its way to public prominence.

While many child therapists tend to avoid forensic involvement, the author of this chapter believes the prevalent practice of noninvolvement in legal proceedings is worthy of reconsideration. From one perspective, many child therapists believe that there are valid clinical reasons for a therapist to avoid court testimony. Maintaining the child patient's privacy is chief among these. Yet, from another perspective, the analytically informed child therapist has particular interview skills that can make a significant contribution to the court's deeper, more thorough understanding of specific issues of children, adolescents, and families. This can affect court decisions in a profound manner. Ethical principles are implicit. Attorneys' requests for assessment of a child may differ vastly from patients who request treatment. The family that is involved in legal battles may seek an advocate within the legal system and the opinions of this advocate may supersede the parent's thinking about the child's need for privacy and confidentiality. It is a delicate balance to serve as an advocate in the legal system and simultaneously engage in that which is therapeutic for a child or adolescent. Yet, in many cases, the analytically trained therapist is in the best position to offer the court an opinion based on the "best interest of the child" (Goldstein, Freud & Solnit 1973). This author does not suggest that the child's therapist function simultaneously as the expert witness for the child and/or family. This would constitute a "dual relationship" and render the therapist ineffective in both roles. It would also raise significant potential for ethical problems.

When assessments for custody cases are performed by therapists who do not have a concept of unconscious conflicts and defenses, reliance upon diagnoses in the *Diagnostic and Statistical Manual* may constitute the entire child evaluation, with little or no attention to that which is below the surface. For this reason, the perspective of the court is influenced solely by matters of cognition, with little attention to unconscious processes, deep and abiding fears and conflicts, and the vicissitudes of the developmental process. One result is that custody decisions may then be based purely upon observable data. Both disciplines suffer and ethical dilemmas are more likely to arise.

While the broad range of ethical imperatives is clearly delineated in the code of ethics that each professional group adopts to serve as guidelines, it cannot encompass every instance that arises. In general, expert witnesses try to address the child's needs and protect the child's vulnerabilities and interests. The expert who is attuned to the inner world of both child and parent can often present a more comprehensive point of view for the court.

With respect to perplexing matters of custody, the medical dictum "do no harm" is frequently invoked. In contrast, another aspect of ethical practice is that of beneficence, which refers to not simply avoiding harm, but actively promoting well being of others. Ethical practices involving children are often viewed through the prism of protecting the patient in the psychotherapeutic experience. From the viewpoint of ethical practice, a child therapist does not establish social relationships with the parents of children whom we treat, and one does not accept forensic or therapeutic cases of persons within the social circle of the therapist. It is unethical to exploit the family financially, to write or discuss the case material without adequate concern for anonymity and consent, or engage in any behavior that endangers or violates the confidential relationship. We recommend to the interested reader chapter 6, on writing clinical material, for more detailed discussion of this subject. Further, ethical practice demands that the child therapist maintain one's competence as a professional and a therapist.

While not a direct ethical concept, there is a tradition among some child analysts and therapists of treating patients gratis or at reduced fees if they lack the means to pay the usual fees. This action on the part of the therapist is consistent with the ethical concept of beneficence. An aspect of ethical practice also involves participation in the public domain, an area in which there is wide variability among child therapists. There is wide variability in terms of the ways in which child therapists are interested in participating in the public domain.

This author became interested in forensic work with children when the director of the St. Louis Institute for Psychoanalysis asked him to participate in a trial. The circumstances were charges brought by a minority physician, who accused his suburban school district of bias and prejudice toward his children, who were the first and only students of this minority group enrolled in the district. After talking to the plaintiff's attorney, who provided background on the legal issues, the author became intrigued by the arguments and decided to become involved. He viewed the legal issue as helping the court to distinguish between the effects of family psychopathology, the effects of the racially biased atmosphere of the school, and the general societal prejudices toward minorities in that particular community.

CONFIDENTIALITY

With respect to both individual treatment and legal proceedings, the subject of confidentiality is more complex in work with children and adolescents than in treatment of adult patients. From a legal standpoint, the child is a minor and can neither request nor relinquish confidentiality. Yet, most child therapists, at the initiation of therapy, explain to the parent(s) the need for the child to have confidentiality protection. What is the essential factor here? If the child trusts her/his therapist implicitly, the child assumes that privacy will be protected. If this trust is ruptured by a court testimony by the child's therapist, thus rendering the child's private statements a part of public record, the resultant breach may make further treatment impossible, with the same therapist or any other.

Many parents understand this concept and are willing to permit the patient/therapist to have a confidential relationship. In some instances parents are skeptical of psychotherapeutic practices of confidentiality, especially when adolescent patients are involved. Parents have widely varying perceptions of what constitutes "acceptable" adolescent behavior and some are reassured only if the therapist agrees to report to them any of the adolescent's deviations from the behavioral, religious, and ethical codes of the parents. If the therapist offers to include parents only in situations in which the behavior is "dangerous" to self or others, the parents may feel too anxious and find the situation untenable. It is a particular challenge to convey the meaning of confidentiality for an adolescent patient to parents who have difficulty in permitting their adolescents to think and act independently.

Many therapists inform the child or adolescent patient that the confidentiality does not mean that parents are barred from hearing about when their child or adolescent is in danger. In such cases, the child or adolescent is told that his/her parents must be involved. One therapist notified the parents that their son "was not to be considered a safe driver." This conversation took place when the son was abusing drugs and driving to his sessions on a major highway twenty to thirty miles-per-hour over the speed limit. The parents interfered with the patient's access to an automobile, and the patient, after an initial angry and vehement denunciation of the therapist, felt reassured by the intervention. The ethical matter here is that the adolescent needs to be informed, early on, that confidentiality is not absolute and that the parent will be informed if the adolescent is placing himself at serious risk. In keeping with our commitment to the adolescent patient, he or she should be informed, prior to the contact with parents that the therapist plans to contact the parents, assuming that the adolescent is unwilling or unable to confront his parents on his own. This is a matter for continuing discussion, in terms of risks, benefits, and principles of ethical practice.

One therapist, early in his career, confronted a crisis concerning confidentiality. During the initial evaluation, the mother of an adolescent boy confided to the therapist that she had lied to her son about the manner in which his father died. She had indicated to her son that his father died in his sleep from a heart attack. In fact, the father had committed suicide, and left a note for his wife. An older sibling of the prospective patient found the note and handed it to his mother. The therapist agreed to protect the mother's communication, unaware of the deep ethical implications of this breach. As the young man's analysis progressed, it became clear that the manner in which he was approaching his commitments was becoming increasingly dangerous. On one occasion he had to be rescued from potentially serious injury by colleagues. When the patient reported a dream about a "piece of paper" that would take a large burden "off his shoulders," his associations lead to his wish to read the note left by this father. As the patient became increasingly insistent about learning the details of his father's communication, his mother asked to meet with her child's analyst. Despite the therapist's emphasis upon the need for the truth so that the child's treatment and, ultimately, his progressive development might continue unimpeded, the patient's mother refused to allow her son to know the truth about his father's death. After seeking consultation, the therapist met with both mother and patient, told them that he was in an untenable situation and could not continue treatment. The therapist then made a referral to another child analyst.

FOR DISCUSSION

- What are the ethical principles in this case?
- What are some of the multiple approaches available to the thoughtful, self-reflective therapist?
- To what degree is the age and developmental phase of the child a consideration in the decision?

- What attention is given to the conflict of the mother over permitting her child to become an autonomous individual?
- How do we work with the parent who is incapable of permitting his/her child to separate and enjoy progressive development?
- What is our ethical obligation to our child patient, who seeks the truth and strives to move ahead developmentally?

When consulting to a university children's hospital, a therapist was approached by a perplexed genetic consultant. During the course of a genetic evaluation of a child, parents, and other family members, it was ascertained that the father of the child was not the biological father. The child's therapist was asked what the geneticist should do with this information. Taking into account the injunction of the Hippocratic Oath to "do no harm," the therapist advised the geneticist to "ignore" the data and simply say that the identified father, along with the other relatives, was not a suitable match. Along these lines, an increasing number of jurisdictions design their laws so that a child born into a marriage is legally the father's child, whether it is genetically accurate or not. This has its roots in English common law, in which the effort was to make every effort to insure that every child would have a father who would support the child, thus avoiding years in the state orphanage. The ethical principles here are complex and may be discussed fruitfully in study groups devoted to this subject.

Challenges to the protection of the child's privacy and confidentiality generally have legal origins, as when parents decide to divorce and one or both of the attorneys want access to the child's psychological treatment records. Often the disputing parties believe that such documents may contain material useful to their client and to the legal resolution of child custody arrangements. In acrimonious divorces it is not unusual for the child to become the "prize" to be won in the legal battle. The parent may assume that, if awarded primary custody of the child, the court has decided that this parent is better, healthier, more devoted, and more caring than the former spouse. It is as though if one "fails" in a marriage, at least one was "successful" as a parent. One can anticipate that the therapist, a transference figure to both child and parents, will experience some pressure to become embroiled in the struggle.

In particular instances the child will have legal representation, namely a guardian ad litem (GAL). While the GAL represents the child legally, their task is also to advise the court on the best legal and psychological alternatives for the child. The appointment of a GAL can be a substantial added cost to litigation. Depending on their training, some GALs will respect the need for the child's therapist to remain outside the conflict. Lacking comprehensive understanding of ethical practices in psychological treatment of children, the guardian may ask to speak "informally." Alternatively, they may subpoena the child's psychological records and wish to have the analyst or therapist deposed. This presents great risk to the child's continuing in treatment, particularly if the therapist complies with the legal requests, thus overriding the child's issues of privacy. Should the therapist enter a request for total confidentiality to preserve the child's trust and treatment by citing our code of professional ethics concerning confidentiality? The child's confidentiality is broken equally if the parent insists that the therapist testify. What if the parents disagree about whether the therapist should maintain the confidentiality of the treatment? One aspect of the crucial ethical question is: To whom does the confidentiality belong?

It is well to remember that one cannot give even a single piece of data to an attorney and then continue to claim confidentiality. From the perspective of the legal system, once confidential information is offered, it then becomes available for *all* inquiries by all parties. Sometimes it is best for the therapist who treats the child of parents involved in legal battles to secure the services of an attorney to deal with these issues as well as to cope with the unexpected subpoenas ordering the production of records or to testify in court.

In some cases a divorcing parent requests that the court allow them to leave the state, often to the city of origin where the parent who is making the petition can more readily find family support and job opportunities. While the analytic literature is divided on the advisability of such an out of state move (Wallerstein and Tanke 1996), the treating therapist may be asked by the court for an opinion in the matter. The ethical question: Should the therapist who treats the child offer an opinion to the court or should this task be that of a therapist or evaluator who takes the responsibility of assessing the child's situation for legal matters? Should both opinions be offered? If a move is involved, what are the implications of disrupting the child's current life, the relationship with the parent who is remaining in this location, and the current treatment? The child analyst or child therapist may have significant data to offer the court in these instances. The overarching rule is to consider which alternative is likely to do the least harm. In general it is best for such testimony to be offered by a forensic evaluator whose purpose is to inform the court.

From an ethical perspective, and that of preserving trust of our patient, the importance of maintaining confidentiality is clear. It is also important to educate parents and attorneys involved in custody of the significance of our stance. When a child therapist whose task is to perform evaluations for court is planning to testify in a particular case, the therapist must clearly inform the parents and child that there is no confidentiality and that anything said may be repeated in the courtroom. When the child is too young or too immature to grasp this, what are our ethical responsibilities? If the analyst or therapist is treating the child and chooses to remain uninvolved in legal proceedings, he or she should engage a psychologically sophisticated attorney in order to "quash" the subpoena that orders the therapist to testify or to open his or her patient's records. It is helpful to be conversant with the U.S. Supreme Court's decision in *Jaffe v. Redmond*. This landmark decision provides legal justification for the therapist's maintaining the confidential relationship with her patient despite an attorney's demands for what might be deemed vital information for his client.

This crucial decision applies only at the federal level. Each state has its own rules about the therapist's privilege to protect patient privacy. In addition to all the confidentiality arguments, it is advisable to emphasize to attorneys that the therapist focuses on the intrapsychic issues so that the he or she may have little data to offer a thoughtful opinion about reality issues. This may be especially pertinent when there have been few meetings with parents during the course of the child's treatment, as in the case of an adolescent. Often the only knowledge that the therapist has of the parents is what the child has communicated and that will be skewed by the stage of the treatment and the prevailing transference issues. This concept, namely changing transferences over time, may require considerable explanation and perhaps even documentation for the insistent, but therapeutically naive, attorney. In essence, while the therapist has complex knowledge of intrapsychic conflicts, the therapist may have little meaningful knowledge of an objective nature to offer the court. While the court and/or attorneys may have difficulty in comprehending this concept, it is the task, from an ethical perspective, of the therapist to inform and to educate them.

There are other instances where the therapist's involvement in court proceedings may be crucial. A senior child analyst was consulted by a child analyst in training about a situation in which a patient's father decided that, after a long absence, he now wanted a relationship with and custody of his son. The particular judge hearing the case seemingly had a bias in favor of fathers, having asserted that contact with the father was essential to heterosexual development and masculinity. Accordingly, both father and judge were intent on accommodating the father's wishes, even though this involved disrupting the boy's relationship with mother, school, friends, and ongoing psychoanalytic treatment. The senior analyst indicated that court testimony might ultimately be most beneficial, even in view of the risk to confidentiality. He suggested that the treating analyst prepare a report for the court, explaining the likely adverse effects of such a drastic upheaval in the child's custodial and geographic status. If the father and the judge were to prevail, and to implement their viewpoint, many significant relationships, including the analytic treatment, would be disrupted, with potential trauma for the child. It may also be necessary to provide the other attorney with relevant articles indicating that the attainment of masculine and gender identity is more complex than simply father presence. There was concern that if the child's analyst had maintained total noninvolvement, it is possible that the child might have experienced this stance as tantamount to neglect and indifference.

Prevention helps. For example, when asked to treat a child whose parents are involved in a contentious divorce proceeding, the therapist needs to be alert to the implications for treatment and discuss the possibility of having one therapist for treatment and another for evaluation for the court. Before agreeing to begin treatment of a child whose parents are embroiled in divorce proceedings, it is advisable for the prospective therapist to ask both parents and their respective attorneys to agree in writing that they will not make any intrusions into the confidentiality of the treatment of their child. The therapist must emphasize the need for a "non-combat zone" without which the treatment is likely to fail. When all agree, it is likely that the child can be treated without legal intrusions.

PROTECTING PRIVACY

In another situation, a pediatrician, as part of routine questioning, elicited from a twelve-year-old, that her father had often sexually molested her. The father confessed and was immediately sent to prison. The father retained a prominent attorney, the mother retained one as well, and the state added its own attorney for "child protection." When the mother asked the therapist to treat her daughter, the therapist asked that all three attorneys honor the confidentiality of the girl's treatment. The mother's attorney agreed, but the other two refused, despite the father's guilty plea. The therapist decided not to treat the child since the circumstances would allow for further intrusions into the privacy of the girl. Her therapist found it paradoxical that the state's attorney, ostensibly beholden to protect the legal interests of the child, would prefer to intrude on her privacy rather than protect her confidentiality.

In a case of contentious divorce, parents brought their child for treatment. The therapist asked that the child's confidentially be protected from legal intrusions, and both parents agreed. Later, the parents reversed their respective decisions and decided that the therapist should testify in court. Although the therapist reminded them of the prior agreement, she was nevertheless served with a subpoena to testify. The therapist retained legal counsel to argue that the therapist should not testify and inwardly was prepared to be in contempt of court. Since the therapist's notes indicated the parents agreed verbally that she not testify, the parents' attorneys stopped insisting upon court testimony. In this case, the therapist had a distinct sense of satisfaction that she had behaved in an ethical manner.

Even in the routine practice of child therapy we are occasionally confronted with a legal challenge that would interfere with treatment. From the viewpoint of the law, when a therapist treats a minor child, the parents are entitled to have access to their child's psychological records. They may even want to use statements made to the therapist by their child to justify and support a custody demand, confirm or deny an allegation of sexual impropriety, or to otherwise use the treatment record for their own personal and/or legal gain. Some therapists resolve this issue by not taking any notes. Others maintain barely adequate record of sessions for the chart and more comprehensive notes for their "personal" use. This "personal record" is analogous to the legal exemption given to a lawyer's "work product," such as notes, references, conjectures, and early formulations that have accumulated over the course of the case. Since the work product may also contain elements of legal strategy, and the results of private investigations, it is protected from disclosure. In a sense, one's personal notes are one's work product, but given a different name so as to coincide with legal terminology. However logical this may seem, the law, once granted access to a therapist's notes will require *all* notes and may not recognize "personal notes." Some may chose to solve this issue by keeping notes to a minimum. Protection of a child's privacy with respect to therapy is an essential matter of ethics. More public awareness is needed, particularly since *Jaffe v. Redmond* is not universally recognized and applies to federal cases rather than to state trials.

With respect to absolute confidentiality offered to patients, state laws vary and we have to be cognizant of the prevailing laws of our own state. While the mandated reporting laws may be necessary and sound in many situations, the therapist needs to use one's best legal and therapeutic judgment in deciding whether to report. For example, an adolescent patient reported to a colleague that his father punched him routinely. The therapist learned that the patient's father had similar encounters, two decades earlier, with his own father. With the patient's permission, the analyst met with the parents and told them that he was a mandated reporter, and that the beating must cease. He indicated that he would not report the current incident, and strongly suggested counseling for the parents. Nevertheless a few weeks later, a teacher noticed some bruises on the adolescent and reported the family. When interviewed by social service workers, the boy denied any parental abuse and the case was dismissed. Motivated to protect his father from embarrassment, the boy also did not want his father to be punished. The adolescent was cognizant of the many adverse consequences of having a parent labeled by the law as "abusive." In this case, we are referring to conscious motivations that impelled the boy to "protect" his father. The treatment revealed significant conflict in this area. While the patient, in a sense, followed the example of his therapist, from the perspective that he did not wish to report his father, the issue was more complex. The therapist decided that his stance was most protective of the boy's progressive development, and appeared, to him, an ethical position. This matter involved transference and countertransference issues as well as legal and ethical ones.

PARTICIPATION IN FORENSIC EVALUATIONS BY A CHILD THERAPIST

Each child therapist and child analyst who participates in forensic work develops effective methods of engagement. In this context, some feel that there is an ethical imperative to participate as "expert" in forensic evaluations for the courts. In many instances, decisions by attorneys, judges, and courts involve children and adolescents. In one example, a father and husband, whose wife had died, was still enrolled in professional school. He asked his deceased wife's sister to take care of his two-year-old daughter, while he finished school in another city. Three and a half years later, the father had graduated, set up his office, and remarried. He sent his wife to the city where his daughter, now five years old, was living with her aunt. His wife was in possession of a writ of habeas corpus which demanded that the aunt produce the child in court. The child's therapist and the aunt retained an attorney who asked an experienced child analyst to testify as an expert.

It is not well-known that one can testify without actually examining the child, since the attorney who wants this particular testimony can present the expert with a hypothetical child who has the characteristics similar to the actual child, and then ask you for expert opinions based on the "hypothetical child." The child analyst who was consulted indicated he would have testified that, considering the suddenness and totality of the change, the child needed a brief period of counseling time and an opportunity to say goodbye to her aunt/mother before she rejoined her father. The judge was dismissive of this position and the stepmother was permitted to walk out of the courtroom with the child. When the child analyst wrote to the judge explaining the child's psychological situation, he received a tersely dismissive comment. Active and prominent participation of well-trained child therapists and analysts, over a sustained period of time, are necessary to offer the viewpoint which grasps and supports progressive development in children.

In spite of the wish of many child therapists to avoid forensic work, there is a tradition, in some areas, to participate actively in ameliorating the suffering of children in whatever setting they are to be found, i.e., schools, reformatories, and court situations, whether they can afford the treatment or are indigent.

TRAINING FOR FORENSIC WORK

The requirement for board certification in this field is one year of training, which may not include careful study of unconscious phenomena, conflicts, defenses, and transferences. Alternatively, the therapist or analyst who is trained in these areas may have a good deal to offer for a child who is engaged in a treatment at the time of court evaluations. The therapist who grasps unconscious dynamics understands symbolism in play, dreams, and fantasies and has an appreciation for the undercurrents of sexuality in the family. He or she knows how to interpret with drawings, doll play, games, and toys, and may know a great deal about the vicissitudes of adolescent sexual and emotional life. While attending to diagnosis, the well-trained therapist grasps family dynamics, the child's psychic position in the family, as well as intrapsychic conflicts. Further it is our custom to think of the continuities and discontinuities of development and to be able to discuss how various impingements skew or otherwise affect various aspects of the child's development and symptoms.

INVOLVEMENT IN FORENSIC ISSUES

When participating in forensic issues, the child therapist must appreciate the differences concerning confidentiality and billing between private/agency practice and forensic participation. In forensics, the rules are somewhat different from in private practice. Similar to clinical practice, one has an hourly rate. When deciding to accept a forensic case, it is best to anticipate, if possible, the amount of work the case will involve, bill accordingly, and secure all or a significant portion as a retainer, before beginning work. Once one has testified and/or submitted a report, the client, from the perspective of an attorney, has no further relationship with the child therapist, except with respect to the final outcome, for which there may be a measure of gratitude. If the result is deemed adverse, it is possible that the therapist's report will be held responsible to some degree, whether or not justified. The other reason for collecting one's fee before court testimony is that the opposing attorney may ask the child therapist how much he or she is being paid for testimony. The implication here is that since the therapist has not yet been paid, he or she is more likely to render an opinion favorable to the retaining attorney. If one's testimony lasts longer than anticipated, an additional bill is appropriate.

Notions of confidentiality in forensic involvement are quite different from what is anticipated in a clinical practice. From the perspective of ethical practice, the child therapist must inform both child and parents that that there is no confidentiality in a forensic interview, and that if there is some issue that they want to keep confidential, they should not discuss it with the therapist conducting the interview for court. Although the child therapist cannot offer confidentiality to anyone in a forensic matter, he or she can use judgment about whether a particular item is sufficiently pertinent to include in a report or testimony. However it is best for the interviewee to recognize that anything said may be repeated in a report or used in testimony.

In summary, the retaining attorney can be helpful not only in preparation of a report but in providing an education about how the law functions. In this piecemeal manner, one gradually acquires knowledge of how legal conflicts are resolved. Awareness of this information allows the child therapist to function in a manner that is consistent with ethical principles.

At times, the expert who is practicing in an ethical manner cannot support the retaining attorney's position. When that is the case, the attorney should be informed early in the case, so that he or she might develop another approach or notify the client that their position is untenable. On the other hand, the attorney may want to retain a different expert, one whose perspective will be more aligned with the client. We are aware that every community has "experts" who will oblige the attorney and defend most any position.

ETHICS AND TESTIMONY

From the outset of a forensic case there may be some positions that are counter to the ethical and/or religious views of the child therapist. For example some would have difficulties in evaluating the allegations of sexual abuse if the alleged offender is an esteemed member of the clergy or a political official. Some would also have difficulty in helping the attorney of an adolescent murderer avoid having his client tried as an adult rather than as a juvenile. Experts need to be aware of their own biases. This, in some respects, is similar to the therapist who needs to monitor and evaluate her/his own countertransferences to the patient. If one thinks that his or her countertransference or ethical principles might distort or interfere with customary objectivity, one should withdraw from the case. On the other hand, if one is passionate about an issue such as the death penalty or abortion, one may choose to work on aspects of his or her own recent divorce or other trauma, or anything that might interfere with the necessary objectivity.

Many child and adolescent therapists view a subpoena with a measure of apprehension and dread, not only because of confidentiality issues, but having to answer questions posed by a hostile attorney who initially will ask questions to which they already know the answers. Their method of operation is to ask what they already know and thus avoid being surprised by what they did not know or expect. In this way, they can guide the judge and jury to see matters from their client's viewpoint. Attorneys vary in their knowledge of psychologically based investigation and/or therapy.

The testifying therapist might want to view this as an opportunity to teach judge and jury the rationale for the therapist's methods of examination, its significance, and how that may be different and in some ways superior, to the opposing expert's presentation. In most instances a testifying "expert" is given great liberties of time to both present and explain the significance of their findings.

The author of this chapter reports that he felt an ethical imperative to use his knowledge and understanding of child analysis and therapy to confront issues in the legal system that potentially could be more "fair" and balanced if the unconscious dimensions of child psychology were addressed and appreciated.

ETHICS AND MISPERCEPTION

There were three issues that based on psychological error, misunderstanding, and misapplication of existing knowledge were causing irreparable harm to innocent people. First was the once widespread use of "anatomically correct" dolls by professionals to diagnose sexual abuse in very young children; second, the application of the dynamics of folie a deux by a prosecutor's office who created credible child witnesses to sexual and physical abuses that I believe never occurred; and lastly, to the later epidemic of "recovery of repressed memory," often initiated by poorly trained therapists, which were used in law suits against clergy and parents.

In the late 1980s, anatomically correct dolls were used by therapists, police, and social service investigators to help ascertain whether children had been sexually abused. Some of the purportedly "anatomically correct" dolls actually had enlarged and prominent sexual organs. After an initial confusion and curiosity, the preschoolers' play involved handling the organs with the dolls, often engaging in aggressive fighting and banging together. This would then be interpreted as representing specific sexual material. At that time, it was thought that the only way a child could be so "sexually knowledgeable" was through actual experience, such as abuse. While some showed caution in interpreting such play as definitive of abuse, for others it identified abuse with certainty.

The fact that all preschoolers are interested in sexual differences and that some may have had primal scene experiences or masturbated with dolls did not enter into thinking or discussion of otherwise thoughtful persons. This author (Shopper 1989, 1991) wrote several letters to the editor cautioning the use of these dolls and questioning their usefulness in a diagnostic assessment of abuse. These letters were noted by the defense attorneys in the Edenton "Little Rascal's" day care trial of Robert Kelly, the husband of the owner of the day care center in North Carolina. Using the theoretical understanding of the dynamics of folie a deux, this author was able to understand how it came about for these children that the fantasies of others, such as accusing parents, prosecutorial staff, four therapists, and a jury, became their reality and thus became credible witnesses for the prosecution (Shopper 2009).

In the early 1990s we had an epidemic of mass hysteria where nursery teachers were accused of sexually abusing their preschoolers. Many were convicted, labeled, and jailed as sexual abusers. One of the "diagnostic tests" of whether a child was sexually abused was to present the child "anatomically correct" dolls and observe how they played with them. Some investigators believed the dolls to be valid tests for determining whether a child had been sexually abused or not. Others felt that the dolls were not valid and that the evaluators totally overlooked the child's existing interest in and knowledge of sexual matters, that they over interpreted the play of the children, and that they should be taken off the market as a diagnostic test. As a child analyst, this author felt it to be not only a scientific issue but also an ethical one (imperative) to forcefully state his views in print and later participate as an expert witness in those court trials.

From an ethical perspective, the crucial issues from those events were that innocent people were serving time in prison, innocent people had their lives and marriages destroyed, based on evidence that may not have been correct. The ethical issue here is that Shopper felt his expertise could prevent harm being done to innocent people. The ethical principle: If knowledgeable people were to simply stand by and watch, ignorance would prevail, and fiction would be accepted as fact.

In the "recovered memory" cases, the author's analytic training and theoretical knowledge was of value in helping courts distinguish between those memories of childhood abuse that was forgotten and/or repressed, in contrast to those individuals who had other motives. There were many people for whom the memories of their abuse were too painful to bear on a daily basis and/or for whom disclosure at the time of the abuse was, for practical purposes, impossible.

FORENSIC INVOLVEMENT IN OTHER AREAS

Termination of Parental Rights

In general, courts are reluctant to terminate parental rights, even when the parent has been absent, abusive, or neglectful. While states vary in their criteria for termination of parental rights, the history of the matter is that the poor, the unmarried, and minority groups are more likely to have their rights terminated in situations of abuse. Part of it may be based in prejudice and a significant part is lack of adequate legal representation. Some parents, although not involved with the rearing of their children, nevertheless refuse to terminate their rights, a process which then enables the child to be legally available for adoption.

The alternative is for the child to remain in the sometimes indeterminate state of foster care. Many states create programs to teach parenting skills with the goal of enabling the parent to attain competence as a parent and so avoid termination of their rights. As a forensic expert in these instances, the author attempted to speak for the child's "best interest," which meant offering opinions on the inadequacy of the parent and/or the program designed to rehabilitate the parent. The obvious problem with these well-intentioned remedial programs is that they are almost entirely cognitively based. They assume that "teaching" how to be a better, more caring parent will overcome the adverse and often traumatic experiences of the biological parent's early childhood. There are few child therapists with an appreciation for unconscious processes who are willing, able, or asked to be involved in the formulation of such remedial programs.

Divorce and Custody Issues

In the context of intense divorce/custody conflicts, charges of child sexual abuse are occasionally directed toward the partner of one of the child's parents. If the court finds credence in these allegations, one parent may have visitation with their children terminated, or have visits supervised by a third party. While these allegations may be constructed by a parent seeking legal advantage, some are authentic. The child therapist can be invaluable to the court in evaluating such allegations.

In other instances the allegations of sexual abuse are directed at a live-in boyfriend or girlfriend that may be valid or concocted. Child therapists, in the course of their clinical practice, develop special skills in interviewing and evaluating the young child. Psychological testing cannot distinguish an abused child from one who suffered trauma in another manner. It is a clinical evaluation to be done with skill and experience, exactly the qualities found in the child therapist who sees young children. While usually we rely on the parent(s) to remember, explain, and interpret a child's experiences and statements, parental opinion in these situations is of little help since each has a huge vested interest in the outcome.

Ethical Issues in Retirement

One crucial area in the work of child therapists, and one that may lead to ethical lapses, involves diminished professional capabilities. We refer to the seriously ill therapist, who may be suffering from a chronic illness, and the aged therapist who believes that his or her thinking is still as acute as ever. Continuing to practice when faced with serious health issues may be related to the economics of retirement, but more important factors are the narcissistic issues inherent in recognizing failing memory, and significant periods of illness and inability to work. As colleagues who often are in a position to observe this decline, what are our professional, ethical, and collegial responsibilities? We are aware that a compromised therapist is not in a position to assist patients. Organizations, training institutes, and colleagues need to address this ethical problem with openness and with respect. Whether there is a committee delegated for this function, or some other administrative arrangement, the issue should not be unacknowledged or overlooked. There is an ethical imperative for each individual to consider the circumstances of his or her plans to discontinue the practice of therapy and analysis.

SUMMARY

Forensic and ethical issues, specific to analytically trained child therapists, are rarely discussed, not because they are of little importance but because those with experience do not address these matters in the literature. As a result, there may be many misconceptions of this work, augmented by an avoidance that is perhaps based more on fantasy than actuality. Our training and understanding, when augmented by some experience, makes us excellent expert witnesses. This chapter is an initial attempt to illustrate how consideration of unconscious processes can be critical in the field of forensic work relating to children, adolescents and their families. The author has emphasized ethical imperatives in contrast to prohibitions and injunctions.

REFERENCES

Amicus brief (2008) in Supreme Court of California Case # S107355, in the marriage of Susan Poston Navarro (LaMusga) and Carry LaMusga.

Goode, E. (2000). The Elian Gonzalez case: The mental health experts: Evaluators are troubled by turmoil around Cuban boy.*New York Times.* April 14.

Goode, E. (2000). The Ellian Gonzalez case: The mental health experts: What a smile hides. *New York Times.* April 26.

Goldstein, J., Freud, A., & Solnit, A.J. (1973). *Beyond the best interests of the child.* New York: Free Press.

Shopper, M. (1989). Letter to editor: The sex abuse controversy. *Journal of the American Academy of Child and Adolescent Psychiatry* 28:5, p. 799.

———. 1991. Letter to editor: Ritual abuse of children. *Journal of the American Academy of Child and Adolescent Psychiatry* 30:6, pp. 1023–24.

———. 2009. What I learned from the Edenton "Little Rascals" sex abuse trial. *Psychoanalytic Inquiry* 29:513–27.

Wallerstein J. S., and Tanke, R.J. 1996. To move or not to move: Psychological and legal considerations in the relocation of children following divorce. *Family Law Quarterly,* 305 cf.

SIX

Write or Wrong? Ethical Considerations in Writing About and Presenting Psychodynamic Work with Children, Adolescents, and their Families

Denia G. Barrett, MSW

The simplest solution to the dilemma of whether or not to write about our clinical work, or to present that work to our colleagues, is to "just say no." There are those therapists who sincerely feel that any writing about what a patient says in a therapeutic context violates a fundamental condition necessary for the process of that work to unfold. Others are comfortable establishing with a patient and/or parents at the outset of their relationship whether or not they may have permission to use clinical examples from their mutual work for educational or scientific purposes as trainees, teachers, or writers. It will not be my aim in this chapter to solve the conflicts every clinician must address each and every time he or she is thinking about writing a paper or making a clinical presentation. Indeed, I believe that the conflicts themselves serve a useful purpose in the maintenance of an omnipresent vigilance and an ingrained and habitual ethical attitude that serve to always place the protection of the patient and the therapeutic work as the first priority.

Concerns about confidentiality and publishing clinical material are not new ones; numerous papers addressing the subject have appeared in professional journals during the past twenty-five years (Clift, 1986; Furlong, 1998, 2006; Klumpner & Frank, 1991; Lipton, 1991; Gabbard, 1997, 2000, 2001; Aron, 2000; Tuckett, 2001; Michels, 2000; Bernstein, 2000;

Coen, 2000; Hartocollis, 2009). Notably absent from the literature, however, have been contributions from those who treat children and adolescents. This may be due to specific emotional factors, including transference and countertransference interferences, that come into play when we contemplate writing about younger patients and that demand different levels of reflection than those that have been raised about using clinical material from work with adults (D. Barrett, 2001; Garber, 1987; Bornstein, 1948). This chapter, like the others in this volume, is meant to serve as a starting point for ethical deliberations. It is our hope that study groups devoted to this topic will abound to add to these initial efforts.

Martin Stein (1988) takes the position that "so long as the writing itself is done with due regard to the conduct of the analysis and the welfare of the patient, it need have no adverse effects on either" (p. 393). His stance suggests a broader approach than the dilemma as posed at the beginning of this chapter; that is, we may ask ourselves not simply *whether* to write about or present clinical work but *why, when, where, about whom,* and *how*. Yet Stein cautions, "We can be sure that our writings, whether or not they include clinical data, have significant and complex meanings for our patients and for ourselves in relation to those patients. To ignore this would be a mistake" (p. 400).

To help reduce the potential for mistakes, the following questions may serve as starting considerations for those whose professional activities include public communications about their clinical work.

- Is this a case that can be considered for presentation or publication at all?
- What motives may be contributing to the idea of using this particular patient's material? At this particular time?
- What mode of sharing clinical material is contemplated? Oral, written, case vignettes, full case history?
- What is the venue? Outside of the therapist's own immediate group, community, state, or country?
- How widely might the written case material be circulated? What is the impact of the internet upon this notion of circulation?
- Should case material be disguised? If so, what methods are preferred?
- Are composites of more than one patient a desirable option in some instances?
- Are publishing without attribution or using a pseudonym as the author viable choices?
- Would coauthoring and combining clinical examples provide greater protection?
- If the case is an ongoing one, will the effect of writing or preparing to present create too much of an interference, whether conscious or

unconscious, in the work? How will the transference be affected if permission is sought?

This list is incomplete and the answer to one question (or inability to answer) will lead to other questions in the process of arriving at ethically reasoned choices regarding writing and presenting. Openly exploring such questions, rather than ignoring them, offers clinicians increased assurance that ethical issues will be accorded a central place in determining how to proceed.

HISTORICAL LEGACY

The first psychoanalytic account of work with an adolescent appeared in 1905, when Freud published a report of his analysis of eighteen-year-old Dora. He admitted at the time that "the presentation of my case histories remains a problem which is hard for me to solve." He recognized that doing so meant betraying secrets which the patient would never give permission to share, but stated his opinion that "the physician has taken upon himself duties not only towards the individual patient but towards science as well; and his duties towards the many other patients who are suffering or will some day suffer from the same disorder." To "avoid causing direct personal injury," he chose to present a patient who was from outside of Vienna, and whose identity as his patient was known at the time to only one other person (his confidant Wilhelm Fliess). He waited four years after the treatment ended and the patient's life circumstances had changed significantly before publishing. "Needless to say, I have allowed no name to stand which could put a non-medical reader upon the scent; and the publication of the case in a purely scientific and technical periodical should, further, afford a guarantee against unauthorized readers of this sort." Finally, he rationalized: "I naturally cannot prevent the patient herself from being pained if her own case history should accidentally fall into her hands. But she will learn nothing from it that she does not already know" (1905 [1901], pp. 7–9).

When Freud published the first case history of child analysis, the case of "Little Hans" (1909a), he used material that had been part of conversations between a father and son. Freud explains in his introduction to the case, "I laid down the general lines of the treatment," and "on one single occasion when I had a conversation with the boy, I took a direct share in it," but otherwise it was a case of "therapy via the parent" (E. Furman, 1969). Freud was again mindful about matters of confidentiality, as he had been regarding Dora, and stated that he owed Hans's father "my sincerest thanks for allowing me to publish his notes upon the case" (p. 5). In a 1922 addendum, Freud wrote to reassure himself and his readers about the breach of privacy:

> When he read his case history, [Hans] told me, the whole of it came to him as something unknown; he did not recognize himself; he could remember nothing; and it was only when he came upon the journey to Gmunden that there dawned on him a kind of glimmering recollection that it might have been he himself that it happened to. So the analysis had not preserved the events from amnesia, but had been overtaken by amnesia itself. (pp. 148–49)

Information about the individual patients described in Freud's case histories subsequently became available through his biographers and the opening of the Freud archives. We can only wonder whether Freud would have decided differently about publishing their analyses if he could have imagined how much about their identities and family circumstances would eventually be revealed. Indeed, the more well-known he became, and the more his patients were apt to recognize one another, the less he wrote about his clinical work. The ethical constraints underwent transformations over time for him, as they do for all of us.

ETHICAL CONSIDERATIONS

As a beginning contribution toward heightening our awareness and sensitivity to these matters, I will use the *Ethics Casebook of the American Psychoanalytic Association* (Dewald & Clark, 2008) and the *Handbook of Ethics of the Cleveland Psychoanalytic Center* (2003) as a framework for identifying and elaborating on those "guiding general principles" that are of particular relevance to ethical decision making regarding clinical writing and presentations of work with children, adolescents, and their parents and other caregivers. A distinct advantage of the latter is that the center's ethics committee includes a number of child and adolescent psychoanalysts and their attunement to the nuanced issues of working with youth and their families is carried through in each section. The source texts use the word "psychoanalyst" throughout, but one may just as well substitute "psychodynamic psychotherapist," as the underlying values are shared among those from multiple professional disciplines. The principles are interrelated and overlap, based as they are on the overarching attitude of respect for the patient. At times they may seem internally inconsistent, for example, when the principle of truthfulness is viewed alongside the concept of disguising material to preserve confidentiality. Such is the nature of ethical struggles and the more deeply one questions, the more complex things become.

The preamble to the *Ethics Casebook* states:

> Psychoanalysis is a method of treating children, adolescents and adults with emotional and mental disorders that attempts to reduce suffering and disability and enhance growth and autonomy. While the psycho-

> analytic relationship is predicated on respecting human dignity, it necessarily involves a power differential between psychoanalyst, patient, and particularly in the case of children, the family that, if ignored, trivialized or misused, can compromise or derail treatment and inflict significant damage on all parties. (p. i)

An asterisk refers to additional text:

> When the patient is a child or adolescent (a minor) the parent(s) or guardian(s) play a significant role in the treatment. In these situations the functions of such a role changes [sic] with age, stage of development, diagnosis, as well as growth of capacity within the patient. How the psychoanalyst relates to the patient and family will reflect such changes. These shifts need to be dealt with in direct and open ways with all concerned. The potential power differential and transference-countertransference between psychoanalyst, patient and parenting figures (or other important family members) can be significant. If not recognized or mishandled such issues can interfere with the treatment and disrupt it. (Dewald & Clark, 2008, p. i)

The editors' emphasis on the impact of unconscious factors, the imbalance of power in therapeutic relationships, and the changes and shifts that occur as a result of interactions between development and therapeutic gains reinforces the need for careful evaluation and re-evaluation of decisions regarding writing and presenting clinical work with our young patients and their families. The ethical principles selected for this chapter can each have particular meanings and pitfalls to consider when thinking about making that private work public.

RESPECT FOR PERSONS

> Psychoanalysts should try to eliminate from their work the effects of biases based on age, disability, ethnicity, gender, race, culture, religion, sexual orientation or socioeconomic class.
>
> —*The Handbook of Ethics of the Cleveland Psychoanalytic Center*, 2003, p. 2

The phrasing of this principle reflects a realistic recognition that however much therapists may try to eliminate the influence of biases from their work, it may never be fully possible. Which biases might come into play when one contemplates presenting or publishing? The age of the patient is one of these, when conscious or unconscious beliefs lead to thinking that a child may be "too young" to understand about such "grown up" matters as professional papers and lectures. The patient may be considered "too little" to be consulted or to have fewer rights regarding confidentiality (B. Bornstein, 1948). The very fact that a child's or adolescent's confidentiality is already compromised to some degree by the therapist's contact with parents may contribute to a loosening of how strictly one views privacy concerns and thus pave the way for too easily dismissing them. On the other hand, distinctions among the concepts of privacy, secrecy, and confidentiality (Novick, J. & Novick, K.K., 2008) may be helpful to one's thinking.

The attitudes one holds about the parents may be another source of potential bias. The extent to which they are viewed as partners in the work may influence whether or not their permission is sought regarding the use of case material. Therapists may have unresolved or unconscious motives relating to telling or concealing secrets from their own parents that can affect their thinking and behavior around presenting work with children and parents.

Respect for the rights and dignity of the patient's siblings or other children who are members of the extended family may dictate whether work involving them is described or omitted in accounts of treatments. Parenthetically, therapists who write about their work with adults who are parents might give careful thought to ethical issues regarding inclusion of material about those patients' children in case presentations.

Racial and socioeconomic biases may operate when determining whether the patient or family would become aware of a publication or presentation. For example, unconscious assumptions about minorities and children and parents from poorer, less financially successful, or less well-educated families might lead to the conclusion that it is "safer" to write about and discuss our work with them because they might be less likely to learn that we have done so. Such false assurances may be grounded in prejudice and can result in taking shortcuts in deciding about the suitability of using clinical material that deny patients equal consideration. Further, circumstances change in unpredictable ways and accessibility to professional literature and announcements of conferences and symposia has become an equal opportunity in this age of the Internet.

Ethnic, cultural, gender, and other biases should all be considered in those instances when a disguise is employed to protect confidentiality. There is a risk of having stereotypes determine how a patient or parent is described, even for those who believe themselves to be free of such influences. Describing a family as "Catholic," "Jewish," or "fundamentalist"—whether factual or disguise—implies a disregard for the individual variations among those belonging to any of those groups. Assigning a nationality can both reflect prejudices of the author and invite those of the intended audience. Even the choice of the pseudonym used for a particular patient can convey unexamined beliefs and attitudes that may reflect bias.

Gabbard (2001) holds that informed consent is necessary when writing or presenting about patients in the mental health field and it is logical to assume that he would advocate for the same approach when it comes to the children of mental health professionals. His caution is well-founded but here, too, a bias may work to discourage a therapist from exploring the matter on the basis of individual circumstances and relationships and to instead dismiss it because the parent belongs to a particular discipline. Valuable material and insights might thereby be unnecessarily lost.

Close attention to these details and having a professional colleague read and edit what one writes can be an aid in meeting the ethical requirement of respect for all persons. It is axiomatic that the manner in which clinical material is conveyed is an indicator of the author's respect, or lack thereof, for the child, parents, and parent-child relationships. A measured, balanced presentation of any material, along with a recognition that parents bring their children to treatment as a way to help relieve their suffering (E. Furman, 1969; K. K. Novick & J. Novick, 2005), demonstrates respect, whether one does or does not have consent.

MUTUALITY AND INFORMED CONSENT

> Psychoanalytic treatment exists by virtue of an informed choice leading to a mutually accepted agreement between a psychoanalyst and a patient or the parent(s) or guardian(s) of a minor patient.
>
> —*The Handbook of Ethics of the Cleveland Psychoanalytic Center*, 2003, pp. 2-3

The question of informed consent is an especially difficult one when applied to writing and presenting work with children and families. Who is to be informed and who can give consent? The child or adolescent? The parent(s) or guardians? All parties involved? The clinical answer to these questions can differ depending on the patient's age or developmental level, and it can change over time. Some candidates and other trainees let the parents of their child patients know that they will present the clinical work to peers, supervisors, and faculty. Other clinicians who regularly write or teach may let parents and older adolescents know they *might* use clinical examples. The latter is a hypothetical communication that can allow a therapist to rationalize that the ethical base has been covered and so avoid any further conundrum. A distinction should be made between getting such a general "informed consent" and seeking specific permission to use material from a treatment relationship for a specific purpose.

Asking a patient's or parent's permission to publish or present can similarly be done *pro forma*—done once, never to be explored again—or it can become part of the process of understanding the patient when a treatment and parent work are ongoing. Any such request will have immediate and long-term consequences at varying levels of consciousness and therapeutic discussion of these should not be foreclosed. When the analyst or therapist requests permission to write or present about the patient's clinical material after a treatment has ended, there will again be both immediate and longer-lasting reactions. In the first case, one imposes something of one's own into the therapeutic world, in the second case one inserts oneself into the patient and family's real world uninvited (Furlong, 2006), with no opportunity to deal with the sequelae over time. A third possibility is one that is not especially unusual for therapists working with children and adolescents. A patient may return at a later age to continue a treatment or for a briefer period of follow-up work, e.g., a patient who finishes in late latency or preadolescence may return during adolescence, or a college student may return for some follow-up sessions. This brings the opportunity to ask how the patient would feel about having the new and/or the previous work published or presented. The same hazard of disrupting the treatment that attends to asking a current patient's permission would apply equally to asking in such follow-up circumstances.

The patient's age, emotional maturity, and relationships with significant others are all factors to weigh in deciding whether or not to ask for consent. The principle of mutuality becomes an important one as it implies that whenever permission is sought, the process should be conducted in a way that allows for the meaningful participation of all parties. The meaning of exposure and giving up of privacy will vary in different phases of treatment and in different developmental phases, as will the patient's impulses to display and reveal.[1] Parents' sense of guilt, shame, or responsibility for a child's problems undergo changes as treatment progresses. Their progress and status in the developmental phase of parenthood alter. Permission given at one juncture might be regretted or withdrawn at another. For patients and parents alike, wishes to please an idealized therapist at one moment might become battlegrounds at another, depending on the transference. Gabbard's (2001, pp. 1083–84) advice to wait to write until after termination offers one solution to these thorny problems. As noted above, however, younger patients not infrequently end one period of treatment and subsequently return for additional therapy later.

The ethical values of mutuality and informed consent may conflict with clinical judgments about the relative harm to the patient or family occasioned by asking permission. These may shift the balance toward proceeding without their knowledge, with measures in place to protect confidentiality. Whether one asks or not, current patients are often attuned to subtle or not-so-subtle signs that something is taking place with regard to their clinical material. Stein alerts us to the fact that the analyst is affected during the process of preparing a presentation and the patient may sense a heightened responsiveness to certain material or symptoms or notice changes in posture, tone of voice, or even what is spread out on the desk (1988, p. 403). Some children may be even more sensitive to these disturbances to the frame, yet less able to put their perceptions into words than an adult patient. Children are, in addition, quite likely to actively snoop by going through the things on the desk or opening up a drawer. Children and adolescents commonly ask whether the therapist takes notes, as they've seen in cartoons. An adolescent who returned for follow-up work was insistent that I had formerly taken notes during his sessions. Although I had never done so, it was my habit to write process notes after all my therapy hours in the expectation that I might write in the future. Parents, too, pick up clues. As I was preparing this chapter and simultaneously contemplating whether to ask a patient's permission to use material for a conference, the patient's mother commented in a parent session, "Maybe you'll write about him one day." Exploring not only the fears but also the wishes to be important or interesting enough to be the subject of a paper is as valuable in work with younger patients and parents as it is with adults.

The sometimes conflicting principles of avoiding exploitation of the patient and responsibility to colleagues in our scientific communities and training institutions, and other patients must be considered as well. Will the patient's or parents' work benefit in any way from the therapist communicating about the work with others in his or her profession, or is the gain solely on the side of the therapist? Will the material add to the cumulative knowledge of the field or simply enhance the reputation of the presenter? Considering the many aspects of these perplexing issues helps us to feel more confident in our decisions but, unfortunately, cannot guarantee the protection the patient and family in every instance.

CONFIDENTIALITY

> If the psychoanalyst uses confidential case material in clinical presentations or in scientific or educational exchanges with colleagues, either the case material must be disguised sufficiently to prevent identification of the patient, or the patient's informed consent must first be obtained. If the latter, the psychoanalyst should discuss the purpose(s) of such presentations, the possible risks and benefits to the patient's treatment and the patient's right to withhold or withdraw consent. In the case of a minor patient, parent(s) or guardian(s) should be consulted,
>
> depending on the age and developmental stage, the matter may be discussed with the patient as well.
>
> —*The Handbook of Ethics of the Cleveland Psychoanalytic Center*, 2003, p. 5

Having discussed informed consent in the preceding section, I will focus here on protecting the patient and family from being identified. Presenting material outside of one's own community can provide some protection but one can never be sure what unexpected connections might exist among patients, families, and the audience. Using vignettes from one or more treatments affords more confidentiality than a case history. Composites of patients with similar difficulties, e.g., children with obsessional symptoms, may be created for certain purposes such as a discussion of technical interventions or theoretical discussions. Neither vignettes nor composites, however, substitute for what can be learned from reports of an individual case. Publishing in professional journals with relatively few subscribers was once assumed to offer reasonable safeguards for such clinical material when it was disguised to some degree.[2]

Disguise has often been recommended as a way to preserve confidentiality but here is what Freud had to say on the matter:

> I have come more and more to regard the distortions usually resorted to in such circumstances as useless and objectionable. If the distortions are slight, they fail in their object of protecting the patient from indiscreet curiosity; while if they go beyond this they require too great a sacrifice, for they destroy the intelligibility of the material, which depends for its coherence precisely upon the small details of real life. And from the latter circumstance follows the paradoxical truth that it is far easier to divulge the patient's most intimate secrets than the most innocent and trivial facts about him; for, whereas the former would not throw any light on his identity, the latter, by which he is generally recognized would make it obvious to every one. (1909b, p. 156)

Further, the use of disguise involves subjective choices on the author's part that can themselves be problematic, as has already been discussed. Common disguises include such things as changes in gender, birth order, or number and gender of siblings. Altering the time frame or location of a treatment, or camouflaging a parent's job are other devices that are employed. One symptom, medical condition, or procedure may be substituted for another. Relatives may be presented as neighbors and vice versa. However, even when a therapist's goal is to stay faithful to the psychically significant and meaningful features of a case, he or she may underestimate the impact of the disguise on the integrity of or scientific value of the case. In the process of reviewing a write-up, it can become clearer that some of the devices or details provided are superfluous and unnecessary for the purpose of the paper or presentation. The help of an editor or advice from a trusted peer can be useful in recognizing when this is the case. Gabbard (2001) points out that disguises can be misleading to colleagues and erroneous assumptions may affect subsequent studies or conclusions, e.g., when a patient is included in a study of psychodynamic therapy and the treatment of children with asthma, when he actually has juvenile diabetes. However useful they may be, disguises are falsehoods and here again one ethical principle, preserving confidentiality, comes into conflict with others—honesty and scientific responsibility. Some authors publish under an acknowledged pseudonym, ("Roberta Green" in Rothstein & Glenn, 1999) and others may choose this option without making it clear that the "author" is fictitious. Others have published without attaching a name to the work. These deceits may provide useful protection for the patient. When, however, they protect the therapist more than the patient, care should be taken so that they do not sidestep ethical qualms and are not part of a rationalization to present something about which one might have too many questions.

TRUTHFULNESS

> The psychoanalyst should avoid misleading patients or parents or guardians of minor patients or the public with statements that are knowingly false, deceptive or misleading.
>
> —*The Handbook of Ethics of the Cleveland Psychoanalytic Center*, 2003, p. 6

Whether a therapist obtains consent or decides against doing so, the issue of truthfulness enters into the equation. Either choice can involve some level of self-deception about what is in the patient's best interests. A writer-therapist withholding the fact that he or she is preparing a paper or talk from a current patient can *feel* deceptive and may thus be affected in the clinical situation and relationships. Obtaining consent does not obviate the need to be ready to respond openly and honestly to patients' and caregivers' questions about the proposed project and to examine their unconscious responses that may have a profound effect upon the treatment.

Robert Furman gave the following description of his direct approach when parents asked him directly if their child would be presented in a group conference:

> After asking what they had in mind, what in effect, their fantasies were, I have said, "Yes, it will be presented to my colleagues because I want their input and to help make certain that I am not missing something that would be helpful for your child. These people are all professionals trained to listen to a case report as if unrelated to any person, leaving the material in the conference room when they leave. They absent themselves if for any reason they feel they could not do that." (1997, personal communication)

In contrast, there may be a tendency to be vague or obfuscate to protect either the patient or oneself. Omitting material out of consideration for the patient or parent may result in a product that is in some ways false, deceptive, or misleading. Leaving out material to avoid the criticism of colleagues or improving upon actual interventions through prose can also be a form of dishonesty, although not necessarily conscious or deliberate. Disguises are, at base, "lies" and the best one might do is to at least be clear in stating that disguises or tricks are being employed.

The ethical requirement of truthfulness applies regardless of the patient's age, but self-scrutiny may reveal a greater tendency to dissemble, hedge, or oversimplify with child and adolescent patients. Misleading oneself may be the biggest obstacle to following the ethical ideal.

SCIENTIFIC RESPONSIBILITY

> The psychoanalyst should take every precaution in using clinical material to respect the patient's rights and to minimize the impact of its use on the patient's privacy and dignity. In the case of minor patients the impact on parent(s) or guardian(s) needs to be considered. Particular care should be exercised in using material from a patient who is still undergoing treatment. It is unethical for a psychoanalyst to make a public presentation or submit for publication in scientific journals falsified material that does not refer to actual observations drawn from the clinical situation. Such clinical material must be disguised sufficiently to protect identification of the patient. The psychoanalyst should exercise caution in disguising patient material to avoid misleading colleagues as to the source and significance of his or her scientific conclusions.
>
> —*The Handbook of Ethics of the Cleveland Psychoanalytic Center*, 2003, p. 9

In an editorial in the *International Journal of Psychoanalysis*, Tuckett speaks to the importance of having access to actual clinical material for establishing criteria for what constitutes "good practice," and as "a major source of new ideas and techniques in psychoanalysis as well as examples for teaching and learning" (2001, p. 1967). In the same volume, Gabbard concludes that "the patient's right to privacy, the profession's requirement to publish advances and new knowledge in the field, and the analyst's need for recognition are inevitably in conflict (2001, p. 1083). Freud spoke of the value of publishing case histories for the welfare of patients in the future. As R. Furman indicates, another way in which patients may benefit from a therapist writing and presenting clinical work is that the feedback from colleagues can improve the work of the presenter or author by offering alternative points of view, pointing out blind spots, or through exchange of thoughts about technique.

Most child and adolescent psychoanalysts see a limited number of young patients because of scheduling constraints, and in many communities they practice in relative isolation (Garber, 1987). These facts of clinical life make it even more important to have the benefit of collective clinical experiences. In addition, the value of child and adolescent psychoanalysis and dynamic psychotherapy is underestimated, underappreciated, and overlooked, even within the broader realm of psychoanalysis. This fact gives added weight to the charge to meet scientific responsibilities by making contributions that demonstrate its efficacy and that add in-depth understanding to the body of knowledge about child development and parent-child relationships, both normal and troubled, typical and atypical.

AVOIDANCE OF EXPLOITATION

> In light of the vulnerability of patients and the inequality of the psychoanalyst-analysand dyad, the psychoanalyst should scrupulously avoid any and all forms of exploitation of patients and their families, current or former, and limit, as much as possible, the role of self-interest and personal desires.
>
> —*Dewald & Clark*, 2008, p. v

As suggested above, the therapist's need or desire for recognition can lead to exploitation of patients and families to satisfy that aim. Child therapists may need to be alert to any tendency to dismiss this potential by rationalizing that the patient "is just a child." Children are vulnerable to being routinely exploited by adults and their psychotherapies should especially protect them from being misused for others' purposes.

An example of this may be Freud's assertion that infantile amnesia prevented the older Hans from recognizing himself in the case history. We do not have sufficient data on what children remember from their treatments to be complacent about infantile amnesia as a protective factor when it comes to publishing and presenting. Parents are often startled by what their children remember at all ages, even if some things remain repressed, and therapists probably get surprised too.

A common element of clinical presentations about children is the inclusion of things that the patient has said or done that elicit pleasure, excitement, mirth, sympathy, or horror in the audience or reader. While full and accurate depictions of how a child works are crucial to good presentations and papers, some descriptions may seduce the audience or interfere with neutral, respectful attentiveness when the "kids say the darnedest things" reaction overshadows the patient. Some cases are so interesting or unusual that the therapist's desire to share them with colleagues may color judgments about consent, confidentiality, or other ethical considerations. Ambition, competition, and exhibitionism may all lead to some degree of exploiting the patient or parents. Stein points out that the therapist gets credited for what was learned in the treatment while the patient usually does not (1988, p. 407). The avoidance of exploitation depends again on the bedrock of ethical decision-making, personal integrity and self-awareness.

PERSONAL INTEGRITY

> Psychoanalysts should strive to be aware of their own beliefs, values, needs and limitations and to monitor how their personal interests impact their work.
>
> —*The Handbook of Ethics of the Cleveland Psychoanalytic Center*, 2003, p. 12

Stein (1988) closes his paper on writing about psychoanalysis by stating that concern over the reaction of the patients [and in the case of children, their caregivers] may adversely affect the quality of what it written, detracting from what might otherwise be a valuable contribution to the field and learning of colleagues. His comment that complex transference and countertransference issues come into play around writing and publishing clinical papers echoes the point of view expressed by the editors of this volume in their introduction. The importance of attending to these matters in the treatment relationship and in the analyst's own "self-scrutiny" is essential, in Stein's view "both for the sake of the analysis itself and what is to be written about it" (p. 408). Earlier he writes:

> Ultimately, the effect of the analyst's writings on the analysis, deleterious or not, will depend not only on what the analyst has written, but to an even greater extend on how his patient has perceived his motives and attitudes. He may view his analyst as sincerely interested in the scientific advancement of psychoanalysis, combining this with clinical concern and personal regard; or he may view him as personally ambitious, self-absorbed, indifferent, and condescending (p. 407).

Both Michels (2000) and Bernstein address themselves to elements in clinical writing that involve "contexts and intentions that are often hidden to the writer as much as to the reader" (Bernstein, 2000, p. 382). The chapter on transference and countertransference in this volume addresses many of the unconscious factors that influence therapists working with children and families. Describing them as unconscious should not imply that these factors are necessarily negative; sound ethical attitudes can come from unconscious identifications with ethical persons in one's personal and professional past, as well as present. Interferences, however, can arise from various intrapsychic sources that have particular pertinence to the process of writing or presenting.

From the realm of the basic strivings and impulses come the competitive and exhibitionistic urges already mentioned. Stein notes that some may write "to impress, please, humiliate or glorify one's analyst" (1988, p. 405) and this may also apply to other significant objects. Voyeuristic tendencies in author and audience may be gratified in the process of looking closely into a case and how it is conducted. Excitement and aggression each play their part in the process of taking a case apart and putting it together in a paper or talk. To the extent that that process is a more or less neutral one, with these factors sublimated in the creative work, these need not be undesirable or disruptive. Signs of areas of difficulty may show in writing about certain aspects of a treatment or being unable to complete a section of a presentation. Paying attention to such problems may provide insight to ethical quandaries which, when addressed, may free the writing from disturbance.

From the realm of affects, pride and pleasure figure prominently for some in writing and presenting the fun and rewards of working with children and adolescents. Pain, distress, and helplessness come with that work too, of course, and the words chosen to convey powerful affects have the power to aid understanding and thinking, or overpower the audience or reader. Erna Furman taught the value of warning listeners if case material might be especially hard to bear, a way of extending the principle of respect for persons to our audience. For some, shame and guilt may be obstacles to honestly bringing forward work from which others might learn. Here I am suggesting that therapists examine not only their eagerness to write but also their reluctance, to determine whether they are living up to ethical standards and obligations.

From the realm of the defenses come the multiple ways in which awareness of ethical lapses can be obscured. Inhibitions and avoidance play a role when therapists do not write. Uncertainties about whether it is wise or appropriate to present certain cases may give rise to denial of potential pitfalls; recognizing and then dismissing concerns can be a negation of them; and to go ahead despite anxiety may involve rationalizations that warrant exploration. Similarly, once a presentation has been made once, it can be all too easy to repeat it or publish it without reconsidering all the implications. Passive-into-active mechanisms may operate when one wants to be the active presenter/writer rather than the passive listener/reader. This again can be both positive and negative, depending on what the material is and how it is presented. Some may shock the audience, repeating the shock they experienced when exposed to primitive material. Others may unconsciously stir feelings of envy, again passing on envious experiences of their own. Still others may want to reproduce the pleasure of receiving clinical material by bringing their own. Any defense available to the personality enters into the process of compiling accounts of clinical work. The question to ask is which effectively serve the purpose of communicating about treatments, and which protect the clinician at the expense of the patient?

The therapist's ego ideal and superego each contribute to efforts to be conscientious and ethical. This discussion of intra-psychic influences would be incomplete, however, if the role of unconscious guilt was not also acknowledged. Conflicts over success can affect the quality of writing or ability to present well. Ethical lapses or compromises might also be a way in which such conflicts find expression.

Posing and answering hard questions is the theme of this chapter. This endeavor begins with a commitment to oneself to try to be as clear-sighted and honest as possible about the ethics involved. The other most valuable advice that can be offered is: When in doubt, request consultation. Seek counsel from colleagues whose own ethical standards and practice have earned your trust.

ETHICAL OBLIGATIONS OF READERS AND LISTENERS

A brief word about the responsibilities of those who receive the case material we offer. At some conferences the registrants are asked to sign a confidentiality statement or a verbal reminder is given at the start of a presentation. Care needs to be taken at meetings where clinical material is presented that discussions do not carry over into the hallways of the building or hotel where the event takes place or continue over dinner with other attendees later that night. If one recognizes any person in a case presentation, the ethical choice may be to leave, as noted by R. Furman above. In addition, Furman expressed the opinion that candidates should be helped to develop a professional compartmentalizing or isolating function that will foster a habit of leaving material where it is encountered, whether in sessions in the consulting room or in meeting rooms (1997, personal communication). Thought needs to be given before referring to case material from others' presentations or papers in written or oral work of one's own. Sharing a paper distributed at a small meeting with a colleague across the country or ocean may seem secure but with every level of wider dissemination, the sense of responsibility to the patient is reduced. Our case material is a precious commodity for training and the ongoing development of our profession and we need to recognize that we have a collective ethical role with all colleagues and patients. There may be times when that role requires us to take concerns to a fellow therapist, in a spirit of helpfulness, when we have heard or read something that could have been presented in an ethically more sensitive manner.

Finally, all of the journals and annuals that exist to provide a home for shared knowledge and experiences related to work with children, adolescents, and parents can benefit from an ongoing effort to ensure that contributors have considered the ethics related to individual cases, and need an evolving review of policies regarding confidentiality to reflect new insights. For example, each periodical can reinforce the importance of confidentiality by requiring a statement from those submitting papers that confidentiality has been safeguarded, by publishing their policy regarding confidentiality in every volume, and by seeking permission from authors with papers in volumes that will be digitized and distributed more widely.

CONCLUSION

The elements of sincere interest in the scientific advancement of our profession, clinical concern, and personal regard are central and fundamental to ethical decision making about communicating clinical material, in any form. In his editorial, Tuckett frames the dilemma by asking how "the ethics of informed consent, the ethics of practice, the integrity of the psychoanalytic setting, and the 'fact' of our need to communicate with each other can be reconciled" (2001, p. 1065).

In my own editorial in 2001 I wrote:

> [T]he very best (and most enjoyable) way to learn about child psychoanalysis is to read what a child and his analyst said to one another as they worked together. New ideas, new techniques, new ways to phrase things in a way that is digestible by a child emerge from such process accounts and can become a part of what one either adopts or rejects for oneself. . . . The "truth" of what we write, insofar as we can know it, should be based on process material. We have an obligation to scrupulously consider and reconsider the issues of confidentiality with every presentation of every patient. We will have to live with some degree of ethical ambiguity, perhaps. At the same time, I submit, that we must "publish or perish" in order to survive as a vital force contributing to the ongoing psychoanalytic understanding and treatment of children, for the benefit of our profession as well as other disciplines related to child development and therapy. More importantly, we must share our work, as Freud said, for the benefit of all patients. (p. 11)

Readers of this chapter may respond to the many caveats regarding the ethics of writing and presenting child psychoanalyses or dynamic psychotherapies by feeling discouraged or put off from the effort. I hope that is not the case for I feel as I did a decade ago, that it is worthwhile to confront the challenges and find ways to write and present that serve our patients, our profession, and ourselves.

NOTES

1. A therapist contemplating giving a workshop to a group of out-of-town colleagues sought consultation about the case and decided to proceed without seeking permission. During the session following the presentation, the adolescent patient whose work had been discussed reported a dream of being in front of a group of people naked. The therapist, struck by the "uncanny" timing of this not-uncommon dream then made the technical choice to respond to it and the underlying fantasies

and wishes, without acknowledging the element of reality that may have reached the patient's awareness. Other technical choices might have had validity as well.

2. The role the Internet has come to play over the past two decades has revolutionized our expectations and ability to find and share information. With the appearance of the Psychoanalytic Electronic Publishing (PEP) in 1998, the full text of over 44,000 articles, fifty-four classic books, and volumes of the Standard Edition became available on line, with frequent new additions (Barrett, 2007/2008). According to Nadine Levinson, of the PEP archive: "PEP is massively visible as we are in the top 75,000 websites in the world (out of literally billions) and our subscriber base is over 7,000 professionals and with eighty universities and growing. We are indexed by Google, thus adding to our visibility. The purpose is outreach and to have psychoanalytic education, research and scholarship available in one spot. Confidentiality is certainly an issue . . . but frankly, once you have published, your clinical material is accessible to someone, somehow" (personal communication). While the editor of a journal with a limited circulation, I was dismayed to discover that volumes were available on eBay and on the shelves of Half Price Books (D. Barrett, 2007/08). Social networking, online games, and other media not yet dreamed of may pose all new hazards for us to discover.

REFERENCES

Aron, L. (2000). Ethical considerations in the writing of psychoanalytic case histories. *Psychoanalytic Dialogues*, 10, (2), pp. 231–45.

Barrett, D. (2001). Publish or perish: An editorial on confidentiality in child analysis. *Child Analysis: Clinical, theoretical, and applied*, 12, pp. 5–11.

Barrett, D. (2007/2008). Child Analysis—A "PEP" talk from the editor. *Child Analysis: Clinical, theoretical, and applied*, 18, pp. 7–10.

Bernstein, S. (2000). Commentary. *Journal of the American Psychoanalytic Association*, 48, pp. 381–91.

Bornstein, B. (1948). Emotional barriers in the understanding and treatment of young children. *American Journal of Orthopsychiatry*, 18, pp. 691–97.

Clift, M. (1986). Writing about psychiatric patients: Guidelines for disguising case material. *Bulletin of the Menninger Clinic*, 50, (6), pp. 511–24.

Coen, S. J. (2000) Why we need to write openly about our clinical cases. *Journal of the American Psychoanalytic Association*, 48, pp. 449–70.

Dewald, P. & Clark, R. (Eds.). (2008). Ethics casebook of the American Psychoanalytic Association. New York: American Psychoanalytic Association.

Freud, S. (1905 [1901]). Fragment of a case of hysteria. In J. Strachey (Ed. and Trans.), *The standard edition of the complete psychological works of Sigmund Freud* (Vol. 7, pp. 7–122). London: Hogarth Press.

Freud, S. (1909a). Analysis of a phobia in a five-year-old boy. In J. Strachey (Ed. and Trans.), *The standard edition of the complete psychological works of Sigmund Freud* (Vol. 10, pp. 5–149). London: Hogarth Press.

Freud, S. (1909b). Notes upon a case of obsessional neurosis. In J. Strachey (Ed. and Trans.), *The standard edition of the complete psychological works of Sigmund Freud* (Vol. 10, pp. 155–318). London: Hogarth Press.

Furlong, A. (1998). Should we or shouldn't we? Some aspects of the confidentiality of clinical reporting and dossier access. *International Journal of Psychoanalysis*, 79, pp. 727–39.

Freud, S. (2006). Further reflections on the impact of clinical writing on patients. *International Journal of Psychoanalysis*, 87, pp. 747–68.

Furman, E. (1969). Treatment via the mother. In A. Katan & R.A. Furman, Eds. *The therapeutic nursery school*, (pp. 64–123). Madison, CT: International Universities Press.

Gabbard, G. O. (1997). Case histories and confidentiality. (Letter to the editor.) *International Journal of Psychoanalysis*, 78, pp. 820–21.

Gabbard, G. O. (2000). Disguise or consent: Problems and recommendations concerning the publication and presentation of clinical material. *International Journal of Psychoanalysis*, 81, pp. 1071–86.

Gabbard, G.O. (2001). Preserving confidentiality in the writing of case reports. *International Journal of Psychoanalysis*, 82, pp. 1067–68.

Garber, B. (1987). The isolation and loneliness of the child analyst. *Annals of Psychoanalysis*, 15, pp. 193–208.

The handbook of ethics of the Cleveland Psychoanalytic Center. (2003). Cleveland Heights, OH: The Cleveland Psychoanalytic Center.

Hartocollis, P. (2009). On publishing ethics: A review of conventions and practices. *Psychoanalytic Quarterly*, 78, pp. 1185–96.

Klumpner, G. & Frank, A. (1991). On methods of reporting clinical material. *Journal of the American Psychoanalytic Association*, 39, pp. 537–51.

Lipton, E.L. (1991). The analyst's use of clinical data, and other issues of confidentiality. *Journal of the American Psychoanalytic Association*, 39, pp. 967–85.

Michels, R. (2000). The case history. *Journal of the American Psychoanalytic Association*, 48, pp. 355–75.

Novick, J. & Novick, K. K. (2008). Expanding the domain privacy, secrecy, and confidentiality. *Annual of Psychoanalysis*, 36, pp. 146–60.

Novick, K. K. & Novick, J. (2005). *Working with parents makes therapy work*. Northvale, NJ: Aronson.

Rothstein, A. & Glenn, J. (Eds.). (1999). *Learning disabilities and psychic conflict: A psychoanalytic casebook*. Madison, CT: International Universities Press.

Stein, M. (1988). Writing about psychoanalysis: II. Analysts who write, patients who read. *Journal of the American Psychoanalytic Association*, 36, 393–408.

Tuckett, D. (2001). Editorial. Reporting clinical events in the Journal: Towards the construction of a special case. *International Journal of Psychoanalysis*, 81, pp. 1065–69.

SEVEN

Common Pitfalls for the Therapist

From the point of view of ethics, there are several common pitfalls for the therapist, but we can prevent ourselves from engaging in problematic behavior if we are consciously aware of following ethical practices in our clinical work. The following are major areas of concern but each therapist must become aware of his or her personal vulnerabilities, which may extend beyond these pitfalls mentioned.

One common pitfall is that of practicing beyond the limits and boundaries of our training, expertise, and competence. Therapists who are trained in psychotherapy with adults, but who do not have training in psychotherapy with children and adolescents, tend to approach therapy with children and adolescents as if they were simply small adults. Thorough knowledge of child development, of the particular conflicts and defenses of children and adolescents, and of techniques appropriate to the child's chronological and maturational age is essential to the ethical conduct of child and adolescent therapy. An example of misapplying techniques appropriately used in work with adults to therapy with children occurs when the therapist interprets the child's actions as merely "acting out" only and thereby misses the communications the child is expressing through the age appropriate mode of action, often used as a precursor to words. For example, the child who engages in "hide-and-seek" play with the therapist is not avoiding putting his or her feelings into words but is showing the therapist in this play complex feelings associated with feeling "lost" and "found," as well as expressing conflicts and defenses over separation and attachment. Work with children and adolescents and their parents presents the therapist with issues, dilemmas, and technical complexities that do not arise in the treatment of adults. The place of the work with parents in the therapeutic frame presents the therapist with complex clinical decisions requiring both training and experience with child and adolescent psychotherapy. Many parents are not aware of the specialized training and skills required to treat children and will select a therapist without this knowledge. Adult patients may ask their own therapist, who is not trained in child work, to evaluate their child. In addition, some child trained therapists find they work more effectively with adolescents than with preschool children and may appropriately limit their practice to adolescents only. The appropriate ethical stance is based on knowing the limits of one's competence and informing the family seeking help that a referral to a therapist trained in child and adolescent psychotherapy is required for optimal treatment.

A significant pitfall is failing to seek supervision or consultation when the therapist is uncertain of his or her interventions, the therapy is at an impasse, when therapy does not progress at an anticipated pace, when acting out on the part of the child is prominent, or when the therapist finds him or herself departing from his or her customary way of working. Persistent anxious or uneasy feelings on the part of a therapist are often warning signals that the therapist would be helped by consultation or supervision with a colleague. This is true of even the most experienced therapists who turn to colleagues with questions about their clinical work. Some therapists are reluctant to seek consultation because of discomfort in revealing their uncertainty or problems to a more experienced colleague. The therapist thinks that he or she should know how to resolve every perplexing issue. The therapist may be concerned that his or her countertransferences are not acceptable or that his or her work may be seen as inadequate. For some therapists, their conflicts around narcissism contribute to a sense of vulnerability, anticipation of criticism and blind spots which prevent them from entering into a consultation focused on understanding the problems in the case at hand. A common example is when the therapist feels that the therapeutic work has reached an impasse. The therapist works to understand the causes of the impasse but the impasse remains resistant to his or her efforts. Rather than seek a consultation to help the therapist with fresh insight into the problem, the therapist may blame the problem on the patient and interrupt the therapy or continue on with ineffective work with the patient. Alternatively, the therapist may become chronically angry with his or her patient and employ interventions that express this affect and are not helpful to the patient. Ethical decisions about an impasse rest on the therapist's understanding his or her blind spots. This is essential to determining whether the impasse stems from the side of the therapist or from the psychological limitations of the patient.

An important pitfall is failing to establish a clear frame for the treatment at the outset of treatment or breaking the frame by the therapist during the treatment. The frame sets the agreed upon practical arrangements and the structure and the expectations for the conduct of the treatment. A rupture of the frame is frequently rationalized as a beneficial shift based on a theory of therapy rather than being perceived as an ethical issue which needs to be understood. Therapists may have difficulty setting the frame at the outset of treatment for fear of scaring the prospective patient and his or her family away. Will the expectations in the frame seem too forbidding, rigid, and impersonal especially during the consultation period when the rapport with the child or adolescent and his or her family is developing? Perhaps the therapist experienced his or her own therapist as being overly rigid and forbidding, so strives to be different with his or her own patients and thus is not clear about the expectations for treatment. This issue is most prominent in setting the fee. Many therapists feel conflicted about discussing the family's financial situation with them and setting a fee. Many fear that the recommendation for treatment involving several hours each week may make the schedule seem impossible. Informing the parents of the therapist's cancellation policy may be an area of conflict for the therapist who anticipates the family will find it too rigid. If the therapist fails to discuss the frame of the treatment in detail the parents may be taken by surprise to learn that cancellations need to be paid for. A difficult problem arises if the parents break the frame by nonpayment of the bill. The agreement about the terms of payment should be established in the frame at the beginning of the therapeutic work. This is an ethical issue because the child or adolescent is vulnerable to financial problems arising between the therapist and the parents or in the family income that could result in the harmful interruption of the child or adolescent's treatment. Parents who become resentful about the fee or negligent in making their payment may stop the therapeutic work for their child abruptly, which is not in the best interests of their child.

With respect to the therapist who deviates from his or her usual ethical practice with the rationalization that "It won't be a problem if I do this just one time" or "It won't matter," this therapist is failing to recognize that the patient and family are vulnerable and sensitive to any unexpected shift in the therapeutic relationship. The therapist is giving insufficient attention to the dictates of his or her conscience and ethical standards. The actions on the part of the therapist set an expectation for the conduct of the treatment. Here the therapist must examine what has blocked his or her conscience from serving as a "road map" for his or her clinical decisions. Examples are breaking confidentiality, accepting a gift, or becoming inappropriately self-disclosing. Touching and other physical contact may begin as seemingly appropriate but can shift in meaning to the child or adolescent as therapy progresses and the child grows, changing from seeking closeness with the therapist to excited overstimulation. When a three-year-old dives into the therapist's lap, he or she may be looking for comfort, but when the adolescent patient seeks opportunities for physical contact, the meanings may be substantively different. The family and patient may think that the change in the frame may now be something to expect as a normal part of the treatment and be puzzled or upset if the therapist acts differently in a later situation. The therapist may rationalize his or her action without considering the developmental age and transferences of the child and may fall into repetitions of an exception to the therapeutic frame, especially if there is unrecognized gratification for the therapist in the exception. Another common example is breaking the confidentiality in the relationship with the child or with the parents. Once the confidential boundary is crossed, the child may lose trust in the therapist and the parents may expect the therapist to reveal the content of the child or adolescent's treatment on a regular basis.

A major pitfall that can lead to ethical infractions is the therapist's failure to be aware of his or her countertransferences and to unconsciously express these in verbal or physical action in the treatment. Therapists may become confused themselves about what is therapeutic and what is "acting out" on the part of the therapist. The introduction of the therapist's personal feelings into the therapeutic process as an acting out or enactment must be differentiated from the therapist's self-knowledge and capacity to use his or her countertransferences in the service of the patient's therapy by increasing understanding of the patient's clinical material. A common example is that of self-disclosure. The therapist may reveal intimate aspects of his or her personal life to the child or adolescent patient or to the family that burden the child, adolescent, or family, thinking that these disclosures provide models for the patient. Sometimes if the therapist and family have had a similar experience, such as a significant loss, the therapist will disclose his or her experience thinking that this expresses empathy for the patient. This often relieves the therapist who may feel pressure to share his or her own loss. More commonly, these disclosures serve to gratify the therapist and may serve as a defense against being the target of the child, adolescent's, or parents' negative affects.

Therapists' narcissistic needs are a major source of ethical lapses, especially when such trends are unconscious. These are observed in the therapist who believes that he or she is the only person who can help the child and his family, thinking that he or she is indispensable. This may lead to inappropriately treating more than one member of the family and failing to refer members of the family as indicated to colleagues. Narcissistic strivings slip into the treatment room as some therapists encourage the child and family to admire and idealize him or her as individuals as well as therapists. This sometimes takes the form of wanting to appear omniscient to the family and failing to appreciate the parental contribution to the treatment process. A common example of the intrusion of narcissistic issues into the treatment is the wish to feel superior to the parents which may result in taking an "expert" and autocratic stance with the parents thus interfering with establishing a working alliance with them. Monitoring our wishes for narcissistic gratification is an important part of our self-observation as is finding narcissistic satisfaction outside the clinical situation.

A common pitfall for therapists is stepping into the parent role with their child and adolescent patients based on the belief that he or she can be a better parent to the patient than the parents themselves. This happens most often when the parental pathology is directly impeding the child or adolescent's normal development. The therapist must remain aware that there are multiple sources of a conscious and unconscious nature such as competitive impulses and unresolved conflicts in the therapist that may lead to this belief. This stance must be differentiated from the therapist's role as a developmental object in the mind of the patient that is appropriate during therapy when the child or adolescent's therapeutic needs are met through this form. It can be quite gratifying to the therapist to see him or herself as a better parent to the child or adolescent's parents as well as to be looked up to and idealized by the patient. The intimate relationship that develops between the child therapist and the child or adolescent can lead the non-self reflective therapist to gradually assume the role of parent. In its benign form, this may pass unnoticed, but may impede treatment when it remains unexamined. The issue of working with acting-out adolescents who are endangering themselves requires considerable skill and self-awareness on the part of the therapist, but this work may be impeded by the therapist taking the role of parent, especially since the adolescent, often unconsciously, views the therapist as a parent. In these situations, the therapist may fear the parents' blame for not stopping their child or adolescent's risky or dangerous behavior and thus depart from a helpful therapeutic stance to an authoritarian position.

A significant pitfall is failure to meet with the parents of the child or adolescent patient in sufficient frequency as is optimal for the patient's treatment. Avoidance of the parents often occurs when the therapist finds the parents challenging, when the therapist responds to the parents with anxiety, or when the parental pathology is severe. Child therapists are often more comfortable with the child or adolescent than with their parents. Resistance to meeting with parents is often rationalized by "they won't come in" or "the father is never available" or "they are so difficult its better to work only with the child." This failure to work with the parents skews the treatment and may lead to failures in understanding the child and adolescent patient as well as hinder the treatment or cause it to be interrupted. In this respect, the therapist may be the one responsible for a "failed" treatment due to his or her conflicts over sufficiently engaging the child or adolescent's parents in a working alliance. A common reason for avoiding seeing the parents is unresolved feelings toward the therapist's own parents. This requires conscientious self-scrutiny and, frequently, consultation. Unresolved anger toward the therapist's parents may be displaced to the mother or father of the patient preventing the establishment of rapport and putting the therapist in an adversarial position to the child or adolescent's parents.

Another pitfall arises from the therapist's failure to understand their legal obligations to his or her patients and their families. Many therapists resist learning about or feel confused by the legal issues commonly met in work with children and adolescents. While there are many ethical and technical issues that arise in relation to the therapist's legal obligations, these cannot be addressed without a firm understanding of the current legal issues. Situations arise in which child-abuse, custody disputes, informed consent, and confidentiality require the therapist to be currently informed about his or her clinical responsibilities in these areas. One common situation is the family that is in the process of a divorce and may expect the therapist to testify in a custody hearing without this being fully discussed by the therapist with the parents at the outset of the case. Another issue is the necessity to be clear with the parents about issues of confidentiality related to requests for information by schools, camps, or insurance forms. Failure to attend to these matters may cause the parents to interrupt their child's or adolescent's treatment to the detriment of the patient.

The proliferation of technology has thrust therapists into new clinical situations that are confusing and the effects on the child and adolescent's treatment are not yet well understood. The use of computers, e-mail, texting, and cell phones impact our work with children and adolescents and their parents. Therapists and patients may become mutually involved with these technologies to the detriment of the clinical work. For example, ethical issues of confidentiality can arise with the use of communication by e-mail. Difficult questions arise in regard to the boundaries of the use of the computer in the therapist's office especially when the child or adolescent wants to watch sexually explicit material or material which may be forbidden by the parents at home. Does the therapist limit the child in conformity to his or her parents' prohibition as well as examining the meaning of the child's wishes to watch prohibited material? This exposes the therapist to ethical dilemmas, sometimes rationalized by viewing these actions as a communication only and ignoring the gratification and stimulation for the child or adolescent patient as well as for the therapist. In addition, the defensive use of cell phones and texting in the therapy hours may not be recognized by the therapist as a defense but accepted as a routine use of these technologies.

The best protections for the therapist against ethical lapses are: conscientious self-reflection and open, searching discussion with colleagues of appropriate ethical principles from the viewpoint of general application and as applied in individual clinical situations. Ethical practice takes place in complex specific clinical moments. We bring our professional ethical stance to these moments. We understand the basis for our ethical decisions most convincingly as we apply our ethical knowledge to daily clinical practice.

Conclusion

The field of mental health is experiencing a surge of interest and activity in the realm of ethical standards. This focuses partially on establishing and enforcing standards of practice through ethics committees. But it is clear that establishing ethical guidelines is only the beginning of integrating articulated standards with clinical practice. Many excellent practitioners in fields of mental health are not always aware of what is expected of them, especially in their legal obligations to their patients. Legal requirements related to mental health practices are frequently changing, thus making it difficult for the practitioner to remain current with the legal obligations of his or her profession. Mental health practitioners are also confronting new ethical issues raised by the entry of various technologies into the therapeutic space and relationships with patients.

Perhaps two factors are of the utmost importance, which bring ethical practice to the forefront of the mental health fields in those areas that pertain to the treatment of children and adolescents. The first is that the therapist practices alone in a room with a child or adolescent patient so the practitioner is left to monitor him or herself. The second is that a child or adolescent patient is especially vulnerable to what the therapist does or does not do. Only the therapist and the child are witnesses to what is happening in the treatment sessions. A child or adolescent is sometimes not believed when reporting an occurrence that would comprise unethical actions on the part of the therapist. The therapist can rationalize, deny, or explain away his or her ethical breach and the therapist's words often take precedence over the patient's version of what occurred. The safety of the therapeutic space for the child or adolescent depends on the ethical conduct of the therapist.

In this book, we thought it was of particular importance to present the positive clinical effects of working within an ethical framework. We have set forth ways in which a professional ethical ego ideal is formed and is maintained. We have emphasized that establishing and maintaining an ethical stance is an on-going developmental task for the practitioner throughout the duration of his or her clinical practice. As we mentioned, unfamiliar challenges for the therapist arise such as in the uses of technology in the therapeutic space. We have set forth our thoughts about what ethical issues are and how they arise in clinical practice with clinical illustrations.

We emphasize that it is insufficient to learn a set of ethical principles or "rules." Ethical decisions are made in clinical moments "on the ground." It is important for the practitioner to have developed his or her ethical understanding and to have internalized ethical principles so that he or she is able to think and act in the clinical moment.

We stress the importance of developing study groups, workshops, and courses on ethics and asking for consultation, all in the interest of developing practitioners' understanding of ethical principles and how to apply them to clinical dilemmas. Ethical theory is not enough; practice in application to actual clinical situations is crucial for the development of an internalized ethical stance and the integration of clinical practice with ethical principles. As we have noted in the text, the practitioner is called upon to make decisions that can reconcile potentially conflicting objectives such as preserving the confidentiality of the child's material while helping the parents understand the problems their child is having.

We have raised as many questions as we have answered. If our volume is taken as a starting point for the development of ethical consciousness in clinical practice we will have fulfilled our purpose.

Appendix

CURRICULUM: ETHICAL PRACTICE IN CHILD AND ADOLESCENT ANALYSIS AND PSYCHOTHERAPY

Session I: What Constitutes Ethical Practice

- The professional ethical ego ideal: formation of and maintaining the ethical stance: personal integrity, personal therapy, theoretical and clinical course work, supervision and learning from experience, self-analysis, consultation and study groups.
- Definitions of boundary violations; boundary crossings; boundary intrusions; enactments.
- Transference-countertransference: a central dynamic underlying boundary issues.
- Therapist's countertransference response to transference and clinical material of the child and adolescent. Pressure on the therapist to regress and its ethical implications.
- Therapist's countertransference response to transferences, dynamics and clinical material in work with parents.
- Therapist's serving as developmental object for the child: confusions and parameters; use and misuse of the concept of the therapist as a real person for the child and adolescent.
- Effects of various theories of what is mutative in the psychotherapeutic treatment of children and adolescents on ethical and boundary issues.

Session II: The Frame and Boundaries in Child and Adolescent Therapy: Essential to Prevention of Ethical Problems

- Establishing the therapeutic frame with the child or adolescent and parents at the outset of treatment.
- Elements comprising the therapeutic frame: for example, consistent length and frequency of sessions, affective constancy of therapist, setting of fees, maintaining boundaries, establishing relationships with the child and the family. How does the therapist present and discuss the frame with the patient and his or her family?
- Techniques and timing for appropriate limit setting for the aggressive, out of control or over stimulated child and adolescent.

- Effects of communication through the child and adolescent's mode of action in the therapeutic process. Potential ethical issues arising from the action mode of expression of affects and conflicts.
- Appropriate behavior for the therapist related to the developmental stage of the child. When is physical contact necessary or appropriate between the patient and the therapist; meaning and ramifications and effects on the transference.
- Transference and countertransference shape the meaning of the therapist's words and actions for the child and adolescent and the parents.

Session III: Parent and Family Work

- The various concepts about and approaches to parent work: effects on the relationship of therapist and parents.
- Confidentiality issues around clinical material from the treatment of the child and adolescent and the work with parents.
- Describe and define the concepts of confidentiality, privacy, and secrecy.
- Respecting privacy.
- Managing family secrets.
- Parent information conveyed to the child and adolescent: when, where, and why.
- Child therapeutic material conveyed to the parents: goals. How to help parents understand their child while preserving confidentiality and respecting privacy.
- Response to request to treat additional family members.
- Protecting the treatment of two family members by two treating therapists.
- Extra-analytic encounters: protecting the patient and family.

Supervisor-Supervisee Relationship

- Ethical issues that arise in the supervisory relationship and why they matter.
- Transferences and countertransferences in the supervisor/supervisee relationship and their impact upon the supervisory process.
- Requests for advice about supervisee's child; requests to treat supervisee's child; conduct in social encounters with the child or adolescent or his or her family.

Common Issues that Enter the Therapeutic Space

- Requests for information from school, summer camp, attorneys and third-party payers.

- Therapist's role in custody issues: protecting the therapeutic work with the child and adolescent.
- Requests to give testimony in court.
- Technology: using the therapist's computer, making cell phone calls, and texting in the hour.
- E-mail communication with parents and child and adolescent: pros and cons.

Presenting and Publishing Clinical Material: Considerations

- How and when to ask permission from the patient and the family to write about their treatment.
- Consideration of the various approaches to presenting and writing about clinical material.

STUDY ISSUES AND QUESTIONS: SAMPLES AND SUGGESTIONS

Session I: What Constitutes Ethical Practice

Questions and Issues for Discussion

1. What conflicts and experiences might interfere with the development and maintenance of a professional ethical ego ideal?
2. Discuss case examples of boundary violations, crossings, intrusions, and enactments.
3. A five-year-old dives into the therapist's lap, or asks to shut off the lights and forbids the analyst to "look," or wants to "dance" with the analyst.
4. What kind of countertransferences might the analyst have in response to this child's behavior?
5. Is this a situation in which the therapist might regress?
6. What are helpful ways to think about the child's requests and how best to respond to them?
7. To what degree might one permit the child to experience a feeling of excitement or danger and then work with the affects therapeutically?
8. At what point does the effective child therapist interrupt this behavior and then work with the child to understand it?
9. What countertransferences might the therapist have toward the adolescent who drapes her body over her chair clearly with a wish to expose her body to the therapist?
10. How would the therapist understand and work with this behavior?

11. What experiences in the therapist's history might make the therapist prone to developing particular transferences to the parents of his patients?
12. Does the therapist consider what might correspond in his or her early childhood to that which took place in the early history of the child patient and or his or her parents?
13. How might an examination of this material in the therapist's personal treatment be of value?
14. How does such symmetry in early experiences lead to "blind spots" in the therapist?
15. Discuss possible countertransference reactions when the child patient's parent is a therapist or is in therapy.
16. Considerations of relationship issues and techniques to avoid boundary issues when the therapist is experienced by the child as a new developmental object.
17. If a therapist is offering a "corrective emotional experience" to the child how does this differ from helping the child or adolescent understand his or her conflicts? Are they simply different theoretical perspectives or might a careful examination reveal deeper meaning?

Session II: The Frame and Boundaries in Child and Adolescent Therapy: Essential to Prevention of Ethical Problems

Questions and Issues for Discussion:

1. How does the therapist introduce the frame to the parents and the child or adolescent?
2. How do the therapist's conflicts affect the effective establishment of the frame with the child, adolescents, and parents?
3. How do we work with the child whose behavior is out of control or dangerous and requires restraint while maintaining appropriate boundaries?
4. Are we more comfortable with the libidinal feelings of our child patients than with his or her negative feelings?
5. Are the libidinal feelings of the adolescent for the therapist easier to accept or do they make us uncomfortable?
6. If so, why is this?
7. Are we comfortable with the child who wants to play ball or hide-and-seek or games of checkers?
8. Is this behavior defensive or is it communicating important conflicts of the child to the therapist?
9. Do we keep urging this child to use his or her words rather than working to understand what the child or adolescent's "action" is telling us?

10. How do we set limits especially when we may be feeling irritated or angry when the child is damaging our office?
11. What kind of physical restraint do we use if necessary?
12. Can we then work therapeutically with the effects of this restraint when the child is able to do so?
13. How do we work with the child about telephone calls from the parents of prelatency, oedipal stage children, and children in stages of latency and adolescence? How does the child's stage of development affect our decisions?
14. Are we listening to how the child, adolescent, or parents may "distort" what we say through the prism of their transferences to us?

Session III: Parent and Family Work

Questions and Issues for Discussion:

1. How does your understanding of the various approaches to family work affect your way of working with families?
2. If the parents of a mid-adolescent whose study habits are compromised call the therapist regularly asking for "reports" on their child, how do we understand this?
3. Do we schedule more frequent meetings with these parents?
4. How do we help these parents understand the importance of confidentiality and protection of the therapeutic space?
5. What if the same issue takes place with a late adolescent, a graduate student whose parents are paying the fee? A young adult?
6. If a parent of a child or adolescent appears at the session and wants to have a "joint session" with the child or adolescent, how is this conceptualized? What responses are respectful of the therapy and of the parent in this clinical moment?
7. How do we respond to parents who want communications with the analyst to which the child or adolescent is not privy?
8. Would you inform a four-year-old that his or her parent notified you of problems at home? Would your stance vary if the child were in latency or adolescence?
9. At what point would you ask the parent to get the child's permission for a consultation with the therapist?
10. How do you handle information that the parent wants to share with the therapist yet keep secret from the child or adolescent patient?
11. Are there any circumstances in which this is advisable?
12. What are the risks to the therapy?
13. What are the countertransference pressures in such cases?
14. What are the ethical and therapeutic considerations of the stance that you elect?

Supervisor-Supervisee Relationship

1. What is the therapist's thinking with respect to ethical principles when asked to treat the child of a supervisee?
2. Of a supervisor?
3. What unique countertransference issues might make such a referral inappropriate?
4. How does consultation help this therapist manage this issue?
5. How does the supervisor work with the supervisee around responses to being asked to treat additional family members or a second child in the family of the supervisee's patient?
6. What are the ethics of treating more than one family member or a sibling of a patient?
7. Discuss the ethics of this issue, particularly with respect to boundaries, transferences, and countertransferences.
8. How does the supervisor help the supervisee to consider the purpose, goals, and risks of conferring with the therapist of a second family member? Under what circumstances might therapists confer when both treat members of one family?

Common Issues that Arise Outside the Therapeutic Hour

1. A child invites the therapist to a Bar/Bat Mitzvah and instructs the therapist: "Don't tell anyone how you got here." Discuss therapeutic modes of working with this material.
2. What if the invitation were to a sports event?
3. Birthday party? Family wedding? Family funeral?
4. Art exhibit or musical performance at which the child longs for the therapist's presence?
5. How does the therapist think with the child about these proposed actions?
6. How might this material be examined therapeutically in contrast to the repetitive response of "What do you think?" which may mean little to the child and not advance his or her thinking?
7. How do we work with extra-therapeutic encounters with our patients: does the therapist bring it up at once in the next hour? Or wait until the patient mentions it? Or ever ignore it?

Requests for Information and the Use and Abuse of Technology

1. When schools, summer camps, and third-party payers request information about our child or adolescent patients do we: share the request with the parents and with the child? If we share the request with the child, at what age and stage of development?

2. The therapist's role in custody issues is first and foremost to protect the child's confidentiality. Should a therapist be involved in testifying when it involves his or her patient? Is treatment viable following such an intrusion? Can this action be worked with therapeutically with the child or adolescent?
3. What are the considerations about using the analyst's computer and cell phone and texting in the hour?
4. Are there therapeutic and boundary considerations?
5. Is it ever necessary to set limits?
6. How do we analyze the meaning of the use of these technologies in the therapeutic space?
7. What are the considerations of communicating by e-mail with parents or child and adolescent patients? What are the pros and cons?
8. What are the ethical concerns when we present or publish clinical material? How do we resolve the conflicting goals of maintaining confidentiality while representing the clinical material accurately?

Index

About the Authors

Anita G. Schmukler, DO, is training and supervising analyst, and supervisor in child analysis at the Philadelphia Center of Psychoanalysis. An active clinician for both adults and children and an esteemed lecturer, she is on the faculties of the Institute for Psychoanalytic Education associated with New York University, the Western New England Psychoanalytic Institute, and the Cincinnati Institute of Psychoanalysis. Dr. Schmukler is also Clinical Associate Professor at the University of Pennsylvania. Her work is published widely and she has edited *Saying Goodbye: A Casebook on Termination in Child Analysis and Therapy.*

Paula Atkeson, PhD, is training and supervising analyst and child supervisor in the Baltimore Washington Institute for Psychoanalysis. She is a faculty member of the Baltimore Washington Institute and has taught at the Clinical Social Work Institute in Washington, D.C. Dr. Atkeson has consulted in several schools in the area and participated in the founding of the Jenny Waelder Hall Center for Children.

Kirsten Dahl, PhD, is a child, adolescent, and adult psychoanalyst in private practice in New Haven, Connecticut. She is a training and supervising analyst at the Western New England Institute for Psychoanalysis and the chair of their Child Analytic Training Program.

Helene Keable, MD, is a training and supervising analyst and a child supervisor at the New York Psychoanalytic Society. She is assistant clinical professor of psychiatry at Mount Sinai Hospital and School of Medicine. Dr. Keable maintains a private practice in child, adolescent, and adult psychiatry and psychoanalysis in New York, New York.

Denia Barrett, MSW, received her training in child and adolescent psychoanalysis at the Hanna Perkins Center for Child Development in Cleveland, Ohio. She served as editor-in-chief of the Center's journal, *Child Analysis: Clinical, Theoretical, and Applied* from 1996 to 2010 and is on the editorial board of the *Psychoanalytic Study of the Child*.

Moisy Shopper, MD, is clinical professor emeritus of child psychiatry and pediatrics at St. Louis University School of Medicine; training and supervising analyst, at St. Louis Psychoanalytic Institute; and Child Adolescent, Adult Psychoanalysis.